Reims & Épernay, France

The Heart of France's Champagne Region

A Starting-Point Guide

Barry Sanders – writing as:

B G Preston

Reims & Épernay, France

ISBN: 9798377586661

1st edition – March 2023-10ba

Acknowledgements: The author greatly appreciates Sandra Sanders' contributions. She provided substantial editorial assistance to ensure the accuracy of this work.

Photography: Photos and maps in the Starting-Point Guides are a mixture of those by the author and other sources such as Adobe Media, Wikimedia, and Google maps. No photograph or map in this work should be used without checking with the author first.

~ ~ ~ ~ ~ ~

Central Reims, the perfect area to relax with a glass of local champagne.

Contents

~ ~ ~ ~ ~ ~

Preface & Overview to this Guide

Introduction & Area Covered:

France's Champagne region is a beautiful sector of France near Belgium and Luxembourg. It is a great area to visit either as a day trip from Paris, or for an extended tour with a stay in the leading towns of Reims or Épernay. These two towns, especially Reims, are central to this guide. Separate chapters are devoted to the highlights of Reims and one on Épernay.

Reims is an easy and relaxing city to explore with broad avenues and excellent transportation.

These are easy towns to explore and provide relaxing stays with many sights right in town. These destinations can each easily be explored in one day. The highlight of the region is, naturally, champagne, its historic and often world-famous houses, and their vineyards.

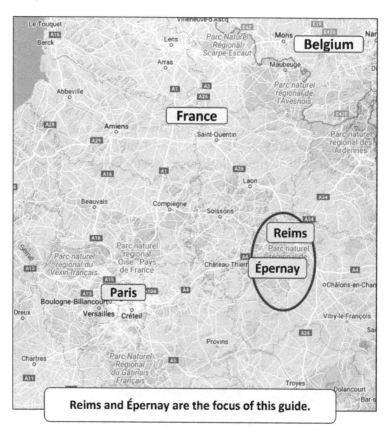

Reims and Épernay are the focus of this guide.

This section of France, the Marne Department, is within the Grand Est region which covers not only the Champagne area but other areas such as the Alsace. This is not a complete guide to all of the Grand Est region or all of the Champagne region as the scope is well beyond the goal of taking relaxing day trips and not wearing yourself down. If you are interested in discovering the Alsace area, a separate Starting-Point Guide is available on Strasbourg and Central Alsace.

Trips into the Champagne region, in addition to tastings which can easily be done in Reims and Épernay, are highly recommended. Numerous tours to the beautiful hilly vineyards are available both from Paris and from the area's cities. Chapter 12 outlines several champagne tour suggestions and companies.

Suggested Itinerary for a Multi-Day Trip:

If your travel schedule allows and you can visit here for more than a day trip **plan on staying at least 2 nights in Reims or 1 night in Épernay.** There is no need to stay in both towns.

Reims & Épernay are home to many of the world's most noted champagnes.

A visit from Paris as a day trip still provides an enjoyable experience. Staying here overnight and adding in a trip to the vineyards along one of the Champagne Routes, is the best way to experience this charming section of France. If you plan on visiting several tasting rooms, it is not necessary to travel out of town but is a joy to do so. To visit wineries outside of town, taking a guided tour is recommended as there is no need to worry about having a designated driver and champagne house visits are included. Without a guided tour, many wineries require reservations.

A two-night itinerary would, for example, allow you to: (a) arrive early or midday on your first day and become oriented to the town you are staying in and then explore some of the top attractions such as the cathedral in Reims; (b) after your first night here, spend a half day touring the vineyards, followed by champagne tastings; then (c) after your second night here, have a relaxing breakfast and head out to your next destination.

Consider an Area Discount Card:

When staying in an area filled with attractions, it can be valuable to purchase a local discount card. In this area, the **"Pass Reims-Epernay"** is offered and gives travelers dis-

counts not only on attractions in Reims and Epernay, but on many area champagne tours as well. (Note, many firms identify and sell this as the **Reims City Card).**

Acquire one if you are likely to visit multiple attractions, area wineries, and take local tours. Do not acquire one if you will only visit one or two attractions during your stay. These passes can always be purchased in the Tourist Offices and are available online prior to your trip.

Age Limitation:

These passes are only available to adults 18 and over.

When visiting here, you will have the option of purchasing this card in increments of 24, 48, or 72 hours. Prices vary by the time of year you will be visiting. See chapter 4 for details on this program or visit the website at **www.Reims-Epernay-Pass.com.**

Visit a Tourist Office:

Both Reims and Épernay have comprehensive websites which provide a wealth of helpful information. In addition, information on tours, lodging and champagne tastings are included.

- Reims: e**n.Reims-Tourisme.com**
- Épernay: **www.Epernay-Tourisme.com**

If you are planning your own tours of the area and want some expert advice that matches your preferences, stopping into one of the area tourist offices is recommended. Both Reims and Épernay have convenient, easy to locate offices.

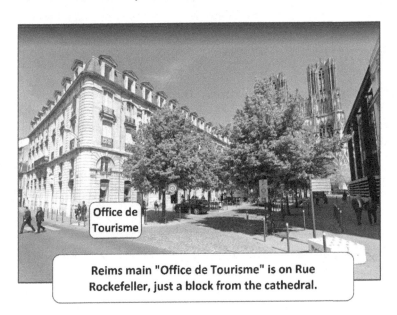

Office de Tourisme

Reims main "Office de Tourisme" is on Rue Rockefeller, just a block from the cathedral.

In the case of Reims, they offer an added service of being able to book a private meeting with one of their advisors in advance. Using this service helps ensure that you will not need to wait in a long line at a service counter.

Reims Tourist Office Locations: Reims is a popular tourist destination and the city provides three offices in town.

- **Main Tourist Office**: Near the cathedral in the heart of Reims. This office is open every day and has the greatest number of services and items for sale. The address is 6 rue Rockefeller, 51100 Reims.

- **Reims Train Station:** In the information center in a small building just outside of the station. It is closed on Sunday and open Monday to Saturday from 1pm to 5pm.

- **Reims and Sillery Marinas**: For individuals who are lucky enough to arrive here by river boat, there is a small branch of the tourist office located on the Canal de la Marne à l'Aisne. It is at the Reims and Sillery Marinas a short distance southeast from central Reims. This office has limited hours and is only open during high season.

Épernay Tourist Office Location: This office, "Office de Tourisme d'Epernay en Champagne," is very central to the town and is directly across the street from the famed Möet et Chandon champagne house and tasting room. If you come by train, the Tourist Office is roughly a 5-minute walk south of the station.

The address is: 7 Av. De Champagne 51200, Épernay.

Understand the local Transportation Systems:

If you are staying in Reims, this small city has an excellent transportation system. The personnel at the Tourist Office will provide you with guidance and maps on how to take advantage of the system. There is no tram or similar system in Épernay, but it is a small town and easy to explore on foot or use the local bus system.

In Reims, in addition to the colorful trams, which extend nearly 7 miles, there are even local tourist buses and rental bicycles available. Chapter 5 provides further details on getting around in Reims. Also, consider downloading one of the many transportation-focused apps for this city and area.

If you purchase a City Card ("Pass Reims-Epernay"), most local transportation is included, making getting around the city even easier.

Reims has a network of brightly colored trams making it easy to navigate the city.
Photo Source: Lunon92 - Wikimedia Commons

Download Some Apps: [1]

With the incredible array of apps for Apple and Android devices, almost every detail you will need for a great trip is available up to and including where to find public toilets. The apps range from those created by official agencies such as the Tourist Office and area train service to several which are put together by individual app developers. Following are a few recommended by the author.

The Reims Tram & Bus Map App

- **Pass Reims Epernay**: Geared toward individuals who purchase this area pass. It details all attractions, tours, and transportation included in the pass. Helpful detailed maps are included.

- **Reims Tram & Bus Map**: Highly detailed maps and schedules for city and area transportation including routes and schedules. A must if you will be using the local transportation system.

- **Explore Reims**: A helpful app for locating area attractions, services, lodging, and more. Good interactive maps which help navigating this city.

---

[1] **Detailed Street Maps Note:** This guide does not include detailed street maps for the simple reason that no printed guidebook or map can be as detailed or interactive as the apps outlined in this guide.

- **France Touristic Travel Guide:** Covers most of France and details the highlights of each city and region. A good app to have if you will be touring several areas.

- **Wine-Explorer:** If you really enjoy delving into the details of wine and champagne, a good idea if you are exploring the Champagne region, this app provides in depth information of French wines and champagne.

- **Rue Des Vignerons:** If you are likely to visit area champagne houses, advance booking is often required. This app enables users to book tours and tastings at many leading champagne houses and other wineries throughout France.

- **Rome2Rio:** An excellent way to research all travel options including rental cars, trains, flights, bus, and taxi. The app provides the ability to purchase tickets directly online.

- **Google Translate:** A must if you do not know any French. This app is a tremendous help when you need to communicate with non-English speaking locals.

- **Trip Advisor:** Probably the best overall app for finding details on most hotels, restaurants, excursions, and attractions.

- **Flush:** A very helpful app which provides guidance on where to find public toilets.

1: The Champagne Region

Unlike many areas in Europe where the primary draw is a specific city and its collection of museums and historical buildings, here, the primary draw is the countryside and its famous product "champagne." The larger towns such as Reims and Épernay are popular destinations, but it is champagne which is the major attraction.

The name "champagne" is synonymous with sparkling wine, and it can be helpful to know that use of this name is strictly limited to wines grown and produced here. The "here" in this statement essentially means in the Champagne region which sits east of Paris. The boundaries of this wine region are strictly defined by French law and there are even five tightly defined geographical subsets. More information on area champagne houses

Much of this area has been designated as a UNESCO Cultural Region for its attractive hillsides and historic champagne houses.

and the delightful champagne routes may be found further in this guide.

The area is characterized by low rolling hills which are dotted with attractive villages and scenic croplands. Wine is not the only crop here as this is a rich agricultural area. The region is, on average, very low in elevation with the altitude of towns such as Reims being only 80 meters (262 feet). Other towns in the region sit at roughly the same elevation. The area only becomes somewhat mountainous when you head east toward the Alsace and head into the Vosges mountains.

Most of Marne and the Champagne area are characterized by low-rolling hills covered in vineyards with attractive villages such as this one next to Épernay.

Area Names & Identities:

There are several identifying names for the area or sections of the region, and it can be confusing. Even names which are no longer official are still often in use casually and will be cited on maps and websites. These identities include:

- Champagne – initially this was the name of a province of France. It has since become a casual identifier for this wine area in general and is no longer a formal geographical area. This name was derived from an early medieval kingdom and covered much of what came to be known as "Champagne-

Ardenne." Historical references cite early spelling as "Champaigne." The simple name "Champagne" is in common usage when it comes to identifying this sector of France.

- Champagne-Ardenne – Up until 2015, Champagne-Ardenne was one of France's administrative regions. In 2015, as part of the consolidation of France's regions (states), it was melded into the much larger Grand Est region of France. The geography of this area is roughly the same as the previously identified province of Champagne. Many maps still show the Champagne-Ardenne sector of France as if it was a formal area, but this is no longer the case.

- Grand Est – France's Champagne growing region sits within the administrative region known as "Grand Est." This is one of 13 such regions within mainland France and, politically, roughly aligns with a state within the United States or a province in Canada. This region was established in 2015 as part of a consolidation of smaller regions and now includes Alsace and Lorraine.

The Grand Est Region of France

- Marne – Marne is one of ten departments within Grand Est with Reims as the largest city and the capital is Châlons-en-Champagne. This area was named for the river Marne which flows through it. **Most of the areas addressed within this guide is in the Marne department.**[2] In population, Marne is the fifth largest department in Grand Est with a total

---

[2] **Geographical Departments in France**: A "Département" such as Marne is a subset of a "Region" which is like a county in the United States. There are currently 96 departments in mainland France.

population just under 600,000 people. Given the agricultural nature of Marne, the population density is one of the lowest in the area.

Other departments in Grand Est include the two Alsace departments of Haut-Rhin and Bas-Rhin, and Ardennes which sits immediately to the north of Marne.

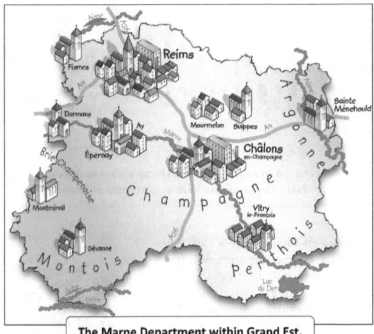

The Marne Department within Grand Est.

Notable Towns in the Marne Department:

Reims: Population of 181,194. When visiting the region for the first time, a visit to Reims with its impressive cathedral is highly recommended. It is also a great small city to use as a basecamp for explorations of the Champagne region if you will be staying overnight. Chapters 5 to 8 of this guide provides further information on Reims, its history, layout, and many points of interest.

Reims is a small city filled with historic sites such as the Place Royale shown here in the center of town.

Châlons-en-Champagne – The capital of the Marne Department, often listed simply as "Châlons," includes Reims and Épernay and many of the leading champagne houses. The population at 44,000 is much smaller than Reims.

There are several notable attractions here including the impressive Saint Étienne Cathedral which was built in the 12th century. Other attractions include the large city hall (Hôtel de Ville) and the ancient city gate "Porte Sainte-Croix" which was

Fun Fact
Châlons is cited as Snoopys crash site after doing battle with the Red Baron.

originally built as a tribute to Marie Antoinette.

Châlons-en-Champagne is on the Marne River which is a popular route for boating. When you visit here, you are likely to see numerous small barges working their way along the river or nearby canals. Boat tours are available, and details may be found at the town's website of: **www.Chalons-Tourisme.com/en**.

Châlons-en-Champagne, an attractive small city on the Marne River.

Épernay – This is the third largest town in the Marne with a population of only 25,000 and it is also the third largest in area. While small, this is a very popular destination for wine and champagne enthusiasts. Several leading brands are headquartered here. In short, if you are coming to the region to enjoy champagne, this should be your top destination.

Chapter 9 of this guide provides insights into the town's layout and attractions.

Reims & Épernay are home to most of the world's top champagne houses.

Other Towns and Getting Around: The above-cited towns of Reims, Châlons, and Épernay are far from the only attractive destinations in the Champagne area. Other beautiful towns which provide enjoyable explorations include Sézanne and Vitry-le-François and charming wine-growing villages such as Cramant.

A big plus to the highlighted towns of Reims, Châlons, and Épernay is they are easy to reach by train or driving and the routes between them are enjoyable. Each of these towns also have great opportunities for wine and champagne tasting.

The map on the next page shows the likely travel time by train between these towns. In each case, the train stations are central to the heart of town and are an easy walk from main attractions, hotels, and shopping. Chapters 5 and 9 provide more information on the town's layouts for Reims and Épernay.

If you spend one or more nights in any of these towns, it is easy to hop aboard a train to visit the other towns for a short trip to do some area and wine explorations.

Traveling to other attractive towns in the area often will require driving, taking a tour, or catching a bus. As a result, they are not detailed here.

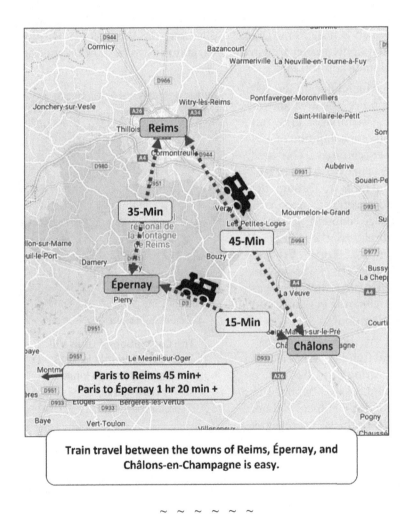

35-Min

45-Min

15-Min

Paris to Reims 45 min+
Paris to Épernay 1 hr 20 min +

Train travel between the towns of Reims, Épernay, and Châlons-en-Champagne is easy.

~ ~ ~ ~ ~ ~ ~

Some History:[3]

Recorded history for Champagne goes back to the 5th century where early chronicles describe an area called Campania, which, in Latin, means "Land of Plains." It was given this name by the Romans due to the similarity with the Italian area of Campania which is near Rome. Around this time, the Romans planted the first known vineyards in the area, taking advantage of the unique climate and soil mix.

Much later, in the 10th century, the area known as Champagne grew out of a consolidation of earlier counties. The area was held by a line of feudal lords up through the 13th century and was large enough to be a threat to the Kings of France, Louis VI and Louis VII. It was only in 1314 that the area was given over to France and King Louis X.

An interesting historical trend developed here starting in 498 when Clovis I was baptized in Reims. Since then, thirty-three monarchs

The Coronation of Louis VIII in Reims Cathedral in 1223. One of 33 French kings crowned here.

---

[3] **Champenois**: When visiting this area, you may come upon the local identifier of "Champenois." This term is used in most cases to identify a language which was once popular in this area, but is now an endangered language. A less formal, but fairly frequent, use of the term is to identify residents of the area.

have been crowned in the Reims Cathedral. (See chapter 6 for an overview of the cathedral and other historical sites of note).

This area was considered to be the frontier of France. Given the easy-to-traverse terrain and proximity to such areas as Belgium and Germany, it has been in the center of many conflicts. Almost every invasion of France has started here. This was especially the case with WWI and WWII. Visitors to the region may visit numerous war memorials and battlefields.

> **The end of WWII**
>
> On May 7, 1945, Germany unconditionally surrendered to the Allies in Reims. The site of this event, a school, is open to visitors.

An interesting attribute of the invasions which occurred here was the ability for both local citizens to take advantage of the many caverns which were used to store and age the local wines.

Since WWII, the popularity of champagne has grown steadily, causing the number of wineries and planted acres to expand. The formal "AOC:" (Appelation D'origine Contrôlée) has grown by 30% since 2008.

2: Traveling to Reims and Épernay

Unless you are taking a Champagne area tour from Paris, your options for traveling to Reims, Épernay, or other cities in the region are essentially limited to taking a train or driving.

Paris is the only city close enough to facilitate easy day trips as many trains will take less than an hour to Reims which is the primary starting point for many. The travel from Paris to Épernay is only

Flying to Champagne
There are no commercial airports here.

slightly longer and there are numerous departures from central Paris each day to both cities. (All trains from Paris to this area depart from the Paris Gare Est station.)

Likely Travel Times to Reims and Épernay				
From	**Travel by Train**		**Driving**	
	Reims - Central	Épernay	Reims	Épernay
Central Paris	50 min	90 min	80 min	90 min
Paris Airport	55 min +	2 hrs +	90 min	95 min
Lille	2 hrs	2 hrs, 20 min+	1 hr 50 min	2 hrs, 15 min

Likely Travel Times to Reims and Épernay				
	Travel by Train		Driving	
From	Reims - Central	Épernay	Reims	Épernay
Strasbourg	90 min+	2 hrs +	3 hrs +	3 hrs, 20 min
Brussels	2 hrs, 40 min +	3 hrs +	2 hrs, 30 min.	2 hrs, 20 min
Luxembourg City	3 hrs	4 hrs	2 hrs, 15 min	2 hrs, 25 min

4

Other "nearby" cities such as Brussels, Strasbourg, or Luxembourg City will all require a minimum of 2 hours travel each way by car or train. Likely travel times are depicted in the above table. This longer travel time is fine if you plan on staying in the Champagne area overnight, but it does not work well with coming here for a simple day trip.

Suggested Travel Planning App:

There are several excellent online sources to help plan your transportation. One of the better firms, which is highly recommended by the author, is **"Rome2rio.com."** This firm provides an excellent website (and app) to use when trying to plan local travel to any city in the Champagne area. It may also be used for almost every city in Europe.

---

4 **Travel Times Notes:** Data source used is **rome2Rio.com**. Driving times are measured from the center of each city. Reims train travel times are measured to the central Gare de Reims and not the Gare de Champagne-Ardenne which sits on the southern outskirts of Reims.

Use this service to view travel options available such as: train, flights, trams, bus, taxi, or self-drive. When choosing bus or train options, the ability to purchase tickets online is available. Schedules for trains and buses are provided with full details.

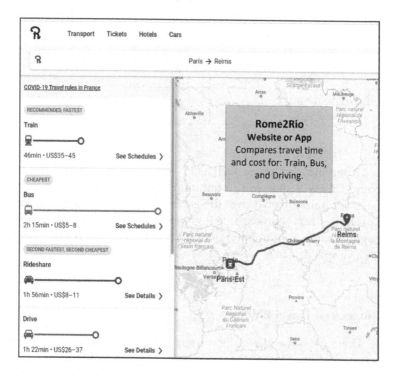

Arriving by Train:

Trains are often the best way to travel to Reims and Épernay, with the one caveat that this mode of travel takes you only to the larger cities and towns. This is not a good way to freely explore the countryside and its many villages and champagne houses.

However, many tours depart from the area's cities making it easy to combine a train trip and an area champagne tour.

If you are traveling from central Paris, all trains to this area depart from the Paris-Est station (which is slightly north of central Paris, despite the "Est" name).

Reims Train Stations:

It is important to note that Reims has three train stations, so some care in making your travel plans is warranted.

- **Gare de Reims** – near the center of town and **recommended** for most travelers. Easily reached from Paris.

- **Reims Maison Blanche** – a neighborhood station south of town. Unless you have plans to visit this part of town, do NOT use this station as it is not convenient for central Reims.

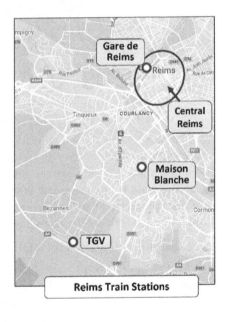

Reims Train Stations

- **Champagne-Ardenne TGV** – located at the southern end of Reims as a station for France's highspeed TGV network. If you are coming from Strasbourg or Nancy, there is a small time savings for traveling to this station, but it is not near central Reims and extra travel into town is required. NOT Recommended for most travelers to Reims.

Reims Train Station / Gare de Reims:

Gare de Reims
Photo Source - Daiima - Wikipedia

The Reims train station is located in the heart of town. It is a small station which is easy to navigate. If you are heading into town and the weather allows, consider walking to the cathedral area. The walk to the cathedral is only 1 kilometer and most of it is along pleasant lanes including the broad Cr. Jean-Baptiste Langlet which follows the tram lines.

Other helpful attributes of this station:

- **Trams**: Several tram lines stop near the front of the train station at the "Gare Centre" stop. The route maps for the trams are easy to find. There is also a helpful app which provides full details on all tram lines in this small city.

> Consider downloading the **Reims Tram & Bus App.** Use it to learn all available routes and schedules.

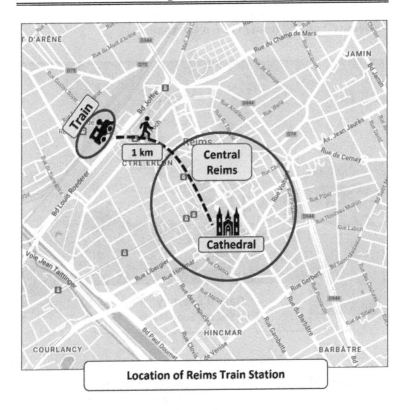

Location of Reims Train Station

- **Rental Cars:** Several leading car rental companies have offices directly outside of this station, including Hertz and Enterprise.

- **Tourist Office:** A small branch of the Reims Tourist Office is located outside of the train station.

- **City Park:** A large set of parks is immediately out front of the train station and includes a carousel for children and outdoor eating opportunities. It is a great place to relax if you have time before catching a train.

Épernay Train Station / Gare d'Épernay:

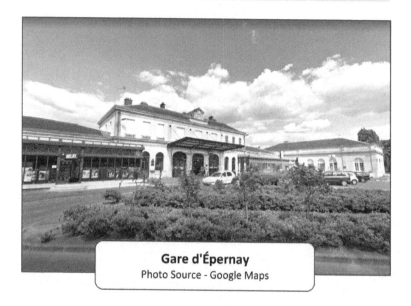

Gare d'Épernay
Photo Source - Google Maps

You could not ask for a better located train station than the small Gare d'Épernay. This station is a short walk to just about everything visitors would want including hotels, shopping, the cathedral, and even some of the world's leading champagne houses.

Unless you are mobility impaired, there is no need to catch a cab or bus from here if your goal is to explore central Épernay. Everything is under a 1-kilometer walk.

If you are looking to travel slightly further out, there are cab and local bus stations immediately out front of the station.

The Épernay tourist office is a six-minute walk due south from the station. This convenient office is also directly across the street from Champagne Moët et Chandon.

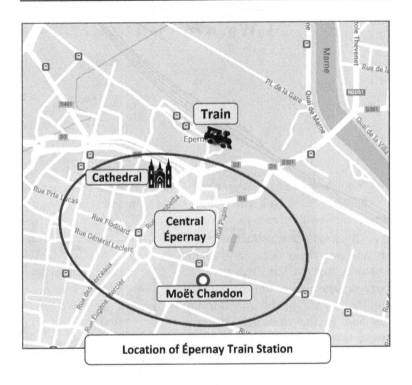

Location of Épernay Train Station

~ ~ ~ ~ ~ ~

3: When to Visit

If you are coming for the champagne experience, the best time to visit here is the Fall. This is **harvest season** and it is when the whole area really comes to life.

This area offers attractive countryside and towns to explore, so it is not necessary to limit travel to the harvest season. In the spring, the rolling hills are filled with wildflowers and in the summer, with the warm days, it is a great area to explore both vineyards and take a walk or bike trip through the area's natural parks.

> Almost any time between early May to the end of October is a good time to explore this area.

Wine tasting can be done at any time as the leading champagne houses (sometimes referred to as champagne cellars) will be open but, if possible, make it fun by coming either during the Fall harvest or visiting one of the area's festivals, many of which occur at other times during the year.

Festivals and Major Events: Leading Festivals in and near Reims and Épernay:

- **Champagne Day:**
    - o <u>When:</u> The 4th Friday of October each year.
    - o <u>Where:</u> There are events celebrating Champagne Day worldwide – as illustrated on the **Champaigne.fr** website. But, well, why not do it right and head to the Champagne

region for this special day where it is celebrated in every town across the region.

- o <u>What</u>: This annual event to celebrate champagne was actually started by a wine blogger in California. It is now a recognized event worldwide with a focus on the Champagne region in France.
- o <u>Website</u>: **ChampagneDay.Champagne.fr**

- **Reims Christmas Market / Le Marché de Noël de Reims:**
  - o <u>When</u>: Late November to Dec 29 – exact dates may vary
  - o <u>Where</u>: Reims – throughout the old town area, near the cathedral.
  - o <u>What</u>: France's 3rd largest Christmas Market with over 125 stalls promoting local foods, crafts regional specialties and, of course, champagne.
  - o <u>Website</u>: Go to the tourist website at **en.Reims-Tourisme.com** – then navigate to the section titled "The Best of Reims."

Reims Christmas Market

- **The Feast of St. Vincent**
  - o <u>When</u>: January 22 each year
  - o <u>Where</u>: Throughout the Champagne region

- o **What:** Annual festivities to thank the patron saint of wine. Each major town in the region will have parades, special church services, and activities.

- Habits de Lumière
  - o **When:** Early December each year – exact dates may vary
  - o **Where:** Épernay
  - o **What:** Come enjoy the light show which occurs prior to Christmas festivals over a 3-day period. Champagne bars can be found throughout town and the light show at night along with livery parades and champagne-centered events.
  - o **Website:** **HabitsDeLumiere.Epernay.fr**

Habits de Lumière - A spectacular lightshow across this attractive town.
Photo Source - HabitsDeLumiere.Epernay.fr

Typical Climate by Month:

Average Area Climate by Month [5]				
Month		**Avg High**	**Avg Low**	**Avg Precip**
Jan	😞	42 F / 6 C	32 F / 0 C	1.8 inches
Feb	😞	45 F / 7 C	32 F / 0 C	1.6 inches
Mar	😐	52 F / 11 C	37 F / 3 C	2 inches
Apr	😐	59 F / 15 C	40 F / 4 C	1.9 inches
May	😊	66 F / 19 C	47 F / 8 C	2.4 inches
Jun	😊	71 F / 22 C	51 F / 11 C	2.2 inches
Jul	😊	77 F / 25 C	55 F / 13 C	2.3 inches
Aug	😊	76 F / 24 C	55 F / 13 C	2.3 inches
Sep	😊	69 F / 20 C	50 F / 10 C	1.9 inches
Oct	😐	60 F / 16 C	45 F / 7 C	2 inches
Nov	😐	50 F / 10 C	38 F / 3 C	1.8 inches
Dec	😞	43 F / 6 C	34 F / 1 C	2.2 inches

[5] **Climate Data Source:** Reims weather as cited in Wikipedia.

4: The Reims-Épernay Passes

If you will be staying overnight in the area and are devoting multiple days to attractions, champagne tastings and tours here, you should consider purchasing an area discount pass.

These passes provide value and convenience **IF** you plan on visiting multiple museums, taking several trips on local transportation, or area tours. They are fairly expensive, so do not purchase one if you will be spending your time simply exploring the town on foot, and only visiting a small number of area attractions.

The pass is available in three timed variations of 24-hour, 48-hour, and 72-hour. The 48- and 72-hour versions cover attractions in both Reims and Épernay. The 24-hour version has the unusual element of requiring you to choose which city you wish to use it in, either Reims or Épernay.

If every case, you must first select the start date for the pass to be used and they are timed from when it is first used on your designated start date. For example, if your first use is at 1pm on a Monday, a 48-hour pass would be good until 1pm two days later.

All passes are limited to adults 18 and over. This works well as it does provide discounts at several champagne houses. Many non-champagne centric activities such as museums are normally free to children.

Pass Prices & Where to Buy:[6]

o   <u>24 –Hour Pass</u>: Reims Pass= € 24 / Épernay= € 19

o   <u>48-Hour Pass</u>: Reims & Épernay = € 36

o   <u>72-Hour Pass</u>: Reims & Épernay = € 42

Given the above pricing, it is easy to see that the cost per day declines with the length of time purchased. This is a savings only if you will be using the pass each of these days.

Where to purchase: The passes are available either directly from the tourist offices while you are in the area or online from several sources including an app.

www.Reims-Epernay-Pass.com

> ### Get the App!
>
> If you download the **"Pass Reims Epernay"** app, you can purchase your passes directly from here. The app provides full details on all free and discounted attractions.
>
> Available in French and English

---

[6] **Pass Prices**: Fees shown here are as of early 2023 and are subject to change. All prices are per adult. No group rate is offered.

Several agencies such as Viator, Get Your Guide, and more also resell these passes. In each case, the firms provide a "mobile ticket" which will be the same download you would get if you were to purchase the pass directly from the app or official Reims-Épernay website.

Caution!

These passes may not be canceled, returned, or have their start dates changed once they have been purchased.

What is Included:

As with most city passes such as these, they include a mix of sites with free entry and other sites or activities which provide discounts to pass holders.

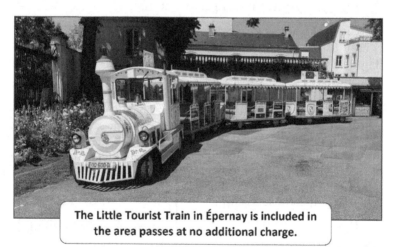

The Little Tourist Train in Épernay is included in the area passes at no additional charge.

Several of the highlights provided as benefits to card holders are in the following list. This is not a complete list as it does change. The recommended app will provide up-to-date details.

Free Items: At the core of the pass are the many free admissions which are provided to pass holders.

- **Museums** – all museums in both Reims and Épernay for 48- and 72-hour pass holders. For 24-hour passholders, this is limited to museums in one of the cities. Chapters 6 and 9 list the museums in these two cities.

- **Public Transportation:** Free use of city transportation such as buses and trams.

- **Tours:** Several free tours including a City Tour in Reims, a Tourist Train in Épernay, a biscuit factory tour, and cathedral tour in Reims. In Reims – you are limited to one free tour of your choice.

Champagne Visits and Tastings: Given that this is the Champagne region, tastings and tours are natural components of an area pass. Numerous local and area cellars, wineries, and restaurants participate and, depending on the location, you will either receive free glasses of champagne or free tours.

	Discounts on Wine Tours	
Several area wine tours provide discounts to travel card holders. Discounts typically range between 10 to 20%.		

In several cases, discounts are also provided on purchases of champagne during your visit. Most of the better-known champagne houses provide benefits to pass holders.

Discounts: In addition to the discounts cited above for champagne tours and tastings, many local businesses and tour operators also provide discounts.

Some discount examples include such delights as a boat tour with lunch, or shop discounts including local chocolate shops, and numerous area restaurants.

5: Reims Overview

Reims has a lot to offer visitors. Although, when making a comparison with leading destinations such as Paris, Bordeaux, or Marseille, this may not seem to be the case. There are several noteworthy sights here but few that stand at the top of leading tourist hotspots in France. This is a good thing as you are not overwhelmed with throngs of tourists following flag-toting guides nor do you have to wait in long lines to view the leading attractions.

Historic Reims and the beautiful cathedral is a great place to start explorations of the Champagne region.

This is a city to visit for casual strolling, enjoying an outdoor café, and delving into the region's specialty, champagne. It is rich in history, ranging from having a cathedral where 33 kings of France were crowned to being the site where WWII officially ended in 1945.

> **Reims has been named "The City of Coronations."**

Reims has been honored twice as a World Heritage Site. In 1991 the city received the honor for the combination of three noteworthy buildings, the Cathédrale Notre-Dame de Reims, the Palace of Tau, and Old Saint Remi Abbey. Each of these locations provides visitors with great experiences and are detailed in the next chapter.

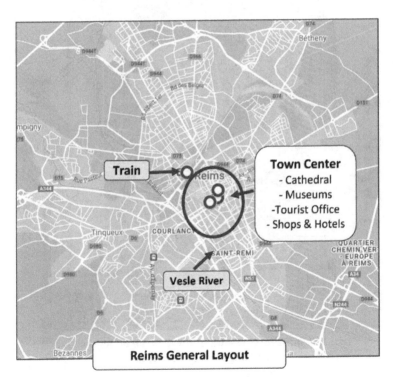

Town Center
- Cathedral
- Museums
-Tourist Office
- Shops & Hotels

Train

Vesle River

Reims General Layout

**The massive Cathédrale Notre-Dame de Reims
dominates the city's skyline.**
Photo Source: Wikimedia Commons

In 2015, Reims was honored by UNESCO again as a World Heritage Site for the Champagne history and landscapes. You don't have to go far to enjoy this history as there are numerous world-renowned champagne houses in the heart of Reims, several of which include intriguing wine caves. Chapter 7 outlines the leading champagne houses in Reims.

Several of Reims more notable **points of interest** are outlined in the following chapter.

In addition to the UNESCO World Heritage Sites, there are options in Reims for a bit of culture or even area sports. Consider exploring the automobile museum here or the Beaux Arts, fine arts, museum.

This is an easy city to navigate on foot and a great destination for a day trip from Paris. One day in central Reims is all that is needed for most visitors to get a good feel for this city and even visit some of the world's leading champagne houses right in town. The historic center is only about 2/3 of a mile across so most sights can be reached on foot in only 15 to 20 minutes.

Getting Around in Central Reims:

Finding your way around in this town is easy. For starters, it is not large and the fact that Reims is on flat land makes navigation very easy.

The cathedral can be seen from almost anywhere in town.

With this great landmark, getting lost just isn't a thing for most people.

Should you desire to use local transportation, there is a surprisingly good network of trams and buses for such a small city. While some streets have cobblestones, for the most part this is minimal and should not be a hindrance for mobility impaired people.

Walking Distances and Times: Most notable destinations in Reims are within a 15-minute walk, as shown below.

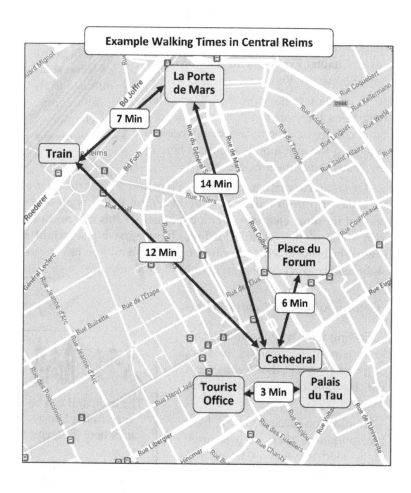

~ ~ ~ ~ ~ ~

Attractions, Champagne Houses & Shopping Areas:

The following chapters provide details on several of the leading attractions such as world-class champagne houses, where to shop and major attractions. To help understand where these destinations are in relationship to each other, the following map and table provide an overview of where they are all in Reims.

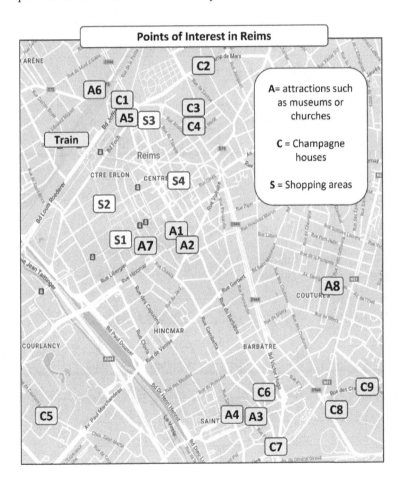

Points of Interest in Reims

A= attractions such as museums or churches

C = Champagne houses

S = Shopping areas

| \multicolumn{4}{c}{**Reims Attractions, Champagne Houses and Shopping Areas**} |
Map Code	Type	Name	Chp
A1	Church	Reims Cathedral	
A2	Museum	Palais du Tau	
A3	Church	Basilica Saint-Remi	
A4	Museum	Saint-Remi Museum	
A5	Roman Monument	La Porte de Mars	6
A6	Museum	Museum of the Surrender	
A7	Museum	Fine Arts Museum	
A8	Museum	Automobile Museum	
C1		Charles de Cazanove	
C2		Maison Mumm Reims	
C3		Champagne Krug	
C4		Louis Roederer	
C5	Champagne Houses	Champagne Lanson	7
C6		G H Martel & Co	
C7		Veuve Clicquot	
C8		Vranken Pommery	
C9		Champagne Ruinart	
S1	Shopping Street	Rue de Vesle	
S2	Shopping Area	Place d'Erlon	
S3	Farmers Market	Halles du Boulingrin	8
S4	Shopping Area	Place du Forum	

Trams & Buses:

Most of the attractions in central Reims and even the leading hotels are within easy walking distance, reducing the need to use local transportation. Some destinations such as the Reims Automobile Museum or the attractions along the river and canal are a bit further afield which will, for most of us, generate a need for local transportation.

The tram system within Reims is surprisingly extensive for a city this size. As cited in the appendix, there are several apps

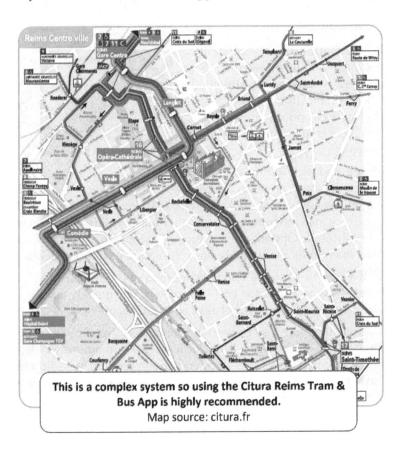

This is a complex system so using the Citura Reims Tram & Bus App is highly recommended.
Map source: citura.fr

available and are highly recommended as full schedules and routes are detailed. Tickets may also be purchased from the app.

Suggested resources to help utilize this system:

Reims Tram & Bus Map App

- Citura website – the firm which operates all public transportation including parking. **www.Citura.fr**

- App – Reims Map & Bus App – detailed routes and schedules.

Ticket Options: For starters, if you have a Reims Pass, there is no need to buy any additional ticket for the duration of your pass as local public transportation is covered by these passes.

All ticket types may be purchased at kiosks near most stops, especially the popular stops within the city center. Tickets cover both buses and trams and there is no need to purchase separate tickets for different types of transportation. Options are numerous, but for casual visitors your most likely choice will be one hour, two hour, or full-day tickets.

If you will likely be taking more than one ride, the full day ticket is suggested as the cost for single tickets quickly adds up. The price for a full day ticket as of early 2023 is only € 4.

Note, there are also the curious versions of "repair" or "troubleshooting" tickets. This is the local system's unique way of letting you purchase a ticket once you are on board if you did not buy a ticket in advance. Costs for these tickets are higher than advance purchase tickets.

Bike Share Service:

A fun way to explore Reims and the champagne area is by bicycle. The city area is largely flat with many broad lanes and perfect for bike riding. An E-bike jaunt over to the river is fun and one of several destinations to consider, such as a ride out to the planetarium.

Zébullo is a city-wide electric bike share service with 25+ stations in central Reims.
Photo source: reims.fr

There are several firms which rent bicycles, and some provide bike tours. For riding in town, one firm to consider is **Zébullo** as they have the most comprehensive bike share service in the area. It operates as many similar bike share services do which allows you to go to one of the area bike share stations, pick out a bike, have a good time, then return it to any station with available slots when you are done.

Using the app is required. The app, the **ZébullO-vélo libre-service**, is available on both the Android and Apple play stores. Once this is done, you need to set up an account, including putting in your payment info. Then, with the app in hand, you can easily locate the bike share stations, available bikes, and also open stations for when you are ready to return the E-bike.

If you wish a more personalized bike experience, different type of bike, or are looking for bicycle tours, the following firms should be considered.

- **Oui Bike**. Operates in Reims and other cities in France. In Reims it is located next to the train station. Several types of bikes are available including E-Bikes, Hybrid, and Mountain Bikes. Their website is **www.OuiBike.net** then go to the page for Reims. If you are coming into Reims by train, their location near the station adds a measure of convenience.

- **CCT Bike Rental** (Cycle Classic Tour). Similar to Oui Bike with the variety of bikes and services, but with the added advantage of a delivery to your lodging service. **www.CCTBikeRental.com**. Then select France and Reims. This firm operates in several countries.

6: Reims Cathedrals & Museums

Visitors to Reims are likely to focus their time on the city's magnificent cathedral and the world-class champagne houses. These destinations are highly recommended, but that is not all there is in this city. There is a variety of sights here ranging from historical monuments such as the Roman Porte de Mars, which requires only a short visit, to large museums such as the Automotive Museum which could take a half day to explore. Nine such sites, including the cathedral, are outlined in this chapter and each can add an understanding of this area and its history.

PASS
REIMS - EPERNAY

This pass should be considered if you are likely to visit several area museums and perhaps also use the local transportation system.

In addition to these historical sites and museums, there are also good shopping and dining areas which can add greatly to the experience. Information on the more popular shopping areas and champagne houses in central Reims is in later chapters.

Every destination outlined here is either within walking distance of central Reims or easily reached by local transportation.

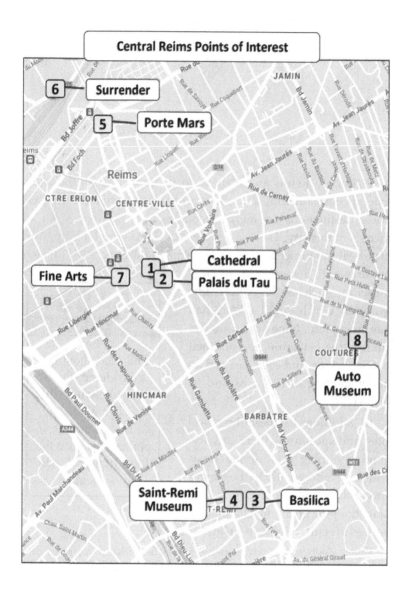

Central Reims Points of Interest

6 — Surrender

5 — Porte Mars

Fine Arts — 7

1 — Cathedral

2 — Palais du Tau

8

Auto Museum

Saint-Remi Museum — 4 3 — Basilica

1 – Cathédrale Notre-Dame de Reims:

Description: Often simply referred to as the Reims Cathedral, this history-laden church is a must-see. If you have time to only visit one attraction in Reims, this should be it. This is a huge structure, standing 266 feet tall and is the most prominent building in the city.

Reims Cathedral

Construction of the cathedral began in the 13th century and work was completed in the 14th century. It is deemed to be a good example of the High Gothic architecture style which was largely centered in northern France. During WWI, it was severely damaged and large sections had to be rebuilt.

The cathedral and its predecessor have been the site for 25 coronations of French Kings, ranging from the first in 1223 to Charles X in 1825. The current cathedral is on the site of the earlier building which had been destroyed.

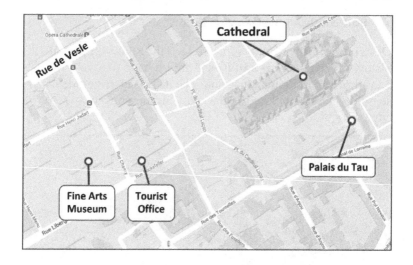

This church is a large complex and much of it is open to visitors. Plan on a minimum of one hour to explore this site. There are many fine elements to this building which can easily be overlooked so joining one of the tours is recommended. Look for such items as: (a) Statues on the front - the Reims Cathedral has more statues on the front façade than any other church in the world; and (b) Champagne Window - inside, there is a large intricate stained-glass window which portrays many elements off the area's history.

Fun Fact

There are over 2,300 statues here.

Cost: As of early 2023, there is an entry fee of € 8 for adults. Free for under 18.

Hours: Normal hours (can vary) are 7:30AM to 7:30PM.

2 – Palais du Tau:

Description: Next door to the cathedral is the king's palace known as "Palace du Tau." This had been the residence of kings during their coronation and it is the former Archbishop's Palace of Reims. Currently, it serves as a museum for the cathedral and houses numerous tapestries and historically important items such as the talisman of Charlemagne.

> **Unfortunately, for all of 2023 and much of 2024, this palace is closed for reconstruction.**

Palais du Tau

~ ~ ~ ~ ~ ~

3 & 4– Basilica of Saint-Remi & Musée Saint-Remi:

Description: In addition to the Reims Cathedral, another magnificent religious structure awaits, the Basilica of Saint-Remi. This is located a bit south of central Reims in the neighborhood of Saint-Remi. This beautiful church is in a complex which includes the Saint-Remi Museum.

Basilica of Saint-Remi Interior

This basilica and museum are listed as a UNESCO World Heritage Site. Built primarily in the 11th and 12th centuries, it contains Saint-Remi's tomb, a huge organ, and a collection of stained-glass windows. During WWI, this was also heavily damaged and reconstruction took over 40 years.

Today, the church and neighboring museum are open to view and guided tours are available. Tours may be booked through the tourist office or the website.

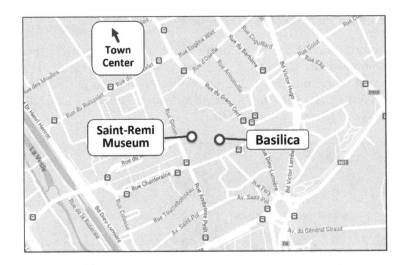

Address: 53 rue Simon, 51100 Reims

Getting Here: This is a little over a mile southwest from the heart of Reims so, if you don't have a car, using the bus system is recommended. The tram lines do not go to this location. There is a "St Remi" bus stop directly out front on Rue Simon.

Cost: If you have a Reims-Épernay pass there is no charge, otherwise, the fee as of early 2023 is € 5,50 for adults.

Hours: Closed Monday. From Tue to Sunday normal hours are 10AM to 6PM for the museum and the basilica. However, the basilica is closed during services.

Website: Use the **en.Reims.fr** site to find current details on both the basilica and the museum.

~ ~ ~ ~ ~ ~

5– Porte de Mars / Mars Gate:

Description: At one point in the Reims history, there were four prominent city gates which led into what was then called "Durocortorum." Built in the 3rd century, the Mars Gate is the only one remaining. It is substantial in size, measuring 32 meters long (104 feet) and 13 meters high, (42 feet).

Porte de Mars - Roman Gate

The arch is free to visit and sits in an open park. For most visitors, it will take only a few minutes to view this historic treasure, but it is worth taking some additional time to view the many carvings which cover this structure.

Nearby and an easy walk, is the Farmers Market, Halles du Boulingrin. In the other direction, is the Surrender Museum, "Musée de la Reddition." One caution, the walk to the Surrender Museum from the Mars Gate is unappealing.

Address: Pl. de la République, 51100 Reims. This is at the northern end of a long park "Les Hautes Promenades" and a short walk from either the train station or Halles du Boulingrin.

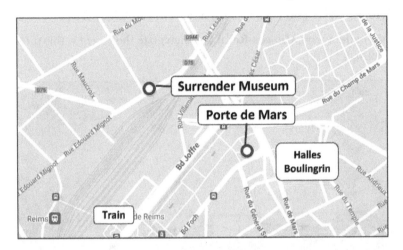

6– Museum of the Surrender / Musée de la Reddition:

Description: Tucked away in an inauspicious building in an un-appealing sector of Reims is the site of the formal end of WWII. In May 1945, General Eisenhower set up the Allied headquarters in a small technical college. On May 7, 1945, the German High Command formally surrendered to the Allies here.

Today, this building is a museum dedicated to this momentous event. Visitors may view the room where the signing took place along with numerous displays and a movie. Allow about one hour to visit here.

> Included in the Reims-Épernay pass.

Address: 12 Rue du President Franklin Roosevelt, 51100 Reims

Getting Here: Take the tram to the Schneiter stop, the same stop used for the Mars Gate, then walk 6 minutes to the museum which is across and over the main rail lines.

Hours: Closed on Tuesday. All other days 10AM to 6PM.

Website: **www.Musees-Reim.fr** – then go to the page for this museum.

The room where WWII ended in the Museum of the Surrender.

7– Fine Arts Museum & Musée des Beaux-Arts:

Description: Unfortunately, as of this writing, the Museum of Fine Arts in Reims is **closed for extensive renovation** and is likely to remain closed until 2025. Further details may be found at **www.Musees-Reims.fr.**

8– Reims-Champagne Automobile Museum:

Description: Sitting in a mostly residential area of Reims is an intriguing museum. It would be easy to pass by as it is in a modest building which does not call out to visitors to stop in and visit. The Reims-Champagne Automobile Museum, or Musée Automobile Reims-Champagne, showcases over 200 classic cars and motorcycles, many dating back to 1908.

View hundreds of classic vehicles in the Reims-Champagne Automobile Museum.

The initial source of the collection came from Philippe Charbonneaux, a noted designer and entrepreneur with a focus on cars and trucks. Almost 200 of the vehicles on display came from him in addition to a collection of over 7000 miniature vehicles.

When visiting here, there is little else in the neighborhood in the way of restaurants, parks, or attractions.

Address: 84 Av. Georges Clémenceau, 51100 Reims. This is roughly one mile southeast from the cathedral, so taking local transportation is recommended if you do not have your own car. There is a bus stop nearby, the Boussinesq stop.

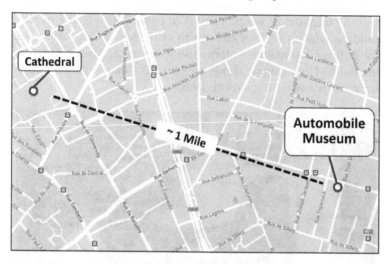

Cost: As of early 2023, the fee for adults is € 10 or € 7,50 for children.

Hours: Closed Tuesday and hours do vary slightly by the season with shorter hours in the winter. During spring and summer, normal hours are 10AM to Noon and 2PM to 5Pm. Note, the museum is closed for a 2-hour lunch.

Website: Musee-Automobile-Reims-Champagne.com.

~ ~ ~ ~ ~ ~

9– Fort de la Pompelle Museum :

Location Note and Area WWI Battlefields: The Fort de la Pompelle is the one museum in this guide outside of the center of Reims. It is included as it provides a great insight into aspects of WWI and the battles which occurred in the region and is near town. Most other notable WWI battlefields are a 30-minute to one hour drive from Reims.

If you wish information on WWI battlefields, cemeteries, and monuments in the area, look into: **www.Greatwar.co.uk**. (Details on these other battlefields are not included as they are outside of Reims and Épernay which is the focus of this guide.)

Tours to WWI battlefields and monuments out of Reims are available. One good resource is: **www.SophiesGreatWar-Tours.com.**

Fort de la Pompelle
Photo Source: Tourisme-en-Champagne.com

Description: This fort, which played a role during WWI, was actually built many years before in 1880 as part of a defensive ring around Reims. During WWI, it was the only fort to not be overtaken and it remained a stronghold of the Allied forces.

Today, this large museum is an impressive showcase for WWI artillery, clothing, hundreds of German army helmets, and even beer steins. This fort was heavily bombed and much of the ground is purposefully kept in this condition.

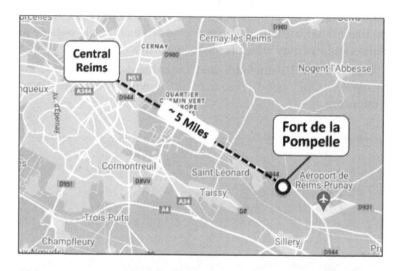

Address: Rd 955, Route de Châlons-en-Champagne, 51100 Puiseulx. Travel by car is required.

Cost: As of early 2023, the fee for adults is € 5,50. Additional fee for guided tours.

Website: **Musees-Reims.fr** – then go to the page for this museum.

7: Reims Champagne Houses

The biggest draw in Reims and the region is understandably champagne and there is a seemingly endless array of champagne houses and boutiques here. **This chapter focuses on nine prominent champagne houses in Reims**. Several, not all, provide tours of their facilities as well.

If possible, don't limit your champagne tasting experience to Reims, even though there is a great variety here. Getting out into the country and traveling through the vineyard covered hills of the area is fun and enlightening. There are hundreds of prominent labels in the area including many smaller operations. Taking one of the many champagne tours out of town or following one of the champagne routes on your own is highly recommended. Chapter 12 provides further guidance on this.

> **Champagne Discounts & Free Tastings**
>
> Holders of the **Reims Pass** will receive either free tastings or discounts on champagne at most area champagne houses.

When coming to Reims, and with the goal of touring the champagne house, it is important to note that **many are open only to pre-arranged groups or by advance reservation**. Joining one of the tour groups, such as those cited in chapter 12, will eliminate this problem. Chapter 12 also provides guidance on booking champagne tastings on your own.

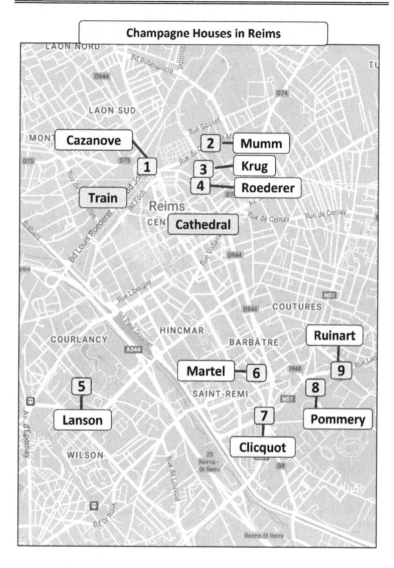

Champagne Houses in Reims

Champagne houses in central Reims are, for the most part, in two clusters: (a) a bit north of central Reims; and (b) a larger grouping closer to the river and canal.

<u>Fun Fact – Cellars & Bottles</u>

Over 150 miles of champagne cellars lie beneath Reims and hold around 200 million bottles of champagne at any one time. The caves were all hand carved out of the chalky soil.

Northern Group of Champagne Houses:

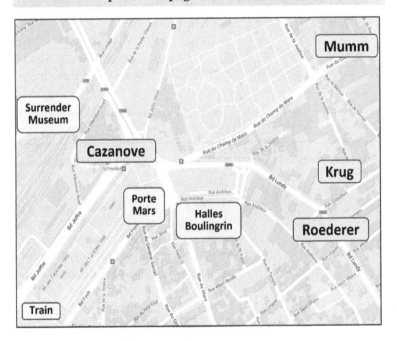

This group of prominent champagne houses offers the advantage of being close to the heart of town. There are other attractions here as well including: Halles Boulingrin farmers market, the roman monument, Le Porte de Mars, and the Museum of the Surrender.

Champagne Houses North of Central Reims	
House/Label	**Address & Details**
Charles de Cazanove	8 Place de la République, 51100 Reims Located close to the Roman gate, Porte de Mars, and easy to reach by tram. This is one of the area's oldest champagne houses. Look for their highly rated Stradivarius Brut. They also produce a well-rated Rosé blend. Tours in English are available and not required in advance. Open daily from 10AM to 7PM with a 1-hour break for lunch. **www.ChampagneDeCazanove.com**
Maison Mumm Reims	34 Rue du Champ de Mars, 51100 Reims The first thing to note when planning a visit is there are two locations – one is a corporate office and the other, with the address cited above, is where to go for visits. The cellars are massive and tours are provided and should not be missed. Advance reservations via their website are suggested and may be done via their website. Closed Saturday and Sunday. Other days, hours are 8:30AM to 6PM **www.Mumm.com**

Champagne Houses North of Central Reims	
House/Label	**Address & Details**
Champagne Krug	5 Rue Coquebert, 51100 Reims One of the world's finest labels, housed in a magnificent mansion with large cellars. Coming here generally requires an appointment and it is often easiest to join a tour group in advance. Drop-in visits are discouraged. For those lucky enough to take a tour, you will be treated to details on the nuances of making fine champagne along with the history of the Krug label. Located just one block from the popular farmers market Halles Boulingrin. **www.Krug.com**
Louis Roederer	21 Bd Lundy, 51100 Reims As with Krug, cited above, just dropping in generally does not work. The best way to visit this top-rated champagne house is with a tour group or making an advance reservation… which their site does not accommodate. Closed Saturday and Sunday. Other days, the hours are 8:45AM to 6PM, closed for lunch. **www.Champagne-Roederer.com**

~ ~ ~ ~ ~ ~

Champagne houses south of central Reims:

Near the river and canal, about a mile south of Reim's historic center, is a large group of notable champagne houses. It is easy to combine a visit to one or more of them with a tour of the Saint-Remi Basilique and accompanying museum. The one exception is the house of Lanson which is across the river and a bit further afield.

Traveling to this part of town will require either driving or taking local buses as the tram lines do not service this area.

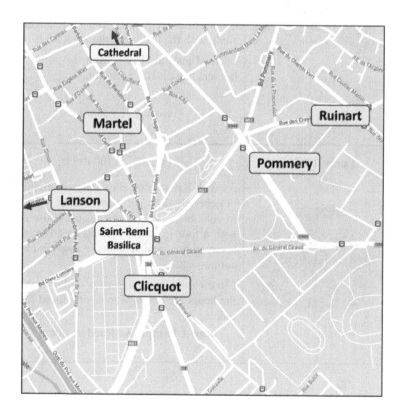

Champagne Houses South of Central Reims	
House/Label	**Address & Details**
Champagne Lanson	66 Rue de Courlancy, 51100 Reims
	Located away from the other champagne houses, and across the river and canal.
	The tours are well rated for their educational quality and they have several tasting packages available. The facility is undergoing renovation in early 2023 and some closures may be encountered.
	Tours available in English and not required in advance. Closed Sunday. Other days open from 8:30AM to 6PM and close for lunch.
	www.Lanson.com
GH Martel & Co	17 Rue des Créneaux, 51100 Reims
	Locations in both Reims and Épernay. The Reims facility is a UNESCO Heritage Site due to its historic and fascinating cellars.
	Noted for their small group tours and advance reservations are not required.
	Well Rated Brute and Brut Rosé wines.
	Open every day from 10AM to 7PM, closed for lunch.
	www.ChampagneMartel.com

| Champagne Houses South of Central Reims ||
House/Label	Address & Details
Veuve Clicquot Ponsardin 	1 Rue Albert Thomas, 51100 Reims Often cited as the best champagne tours and facilities to visit in Reims. Very popular destination and the extensive cave is classified as a UNESCO World Heritage Site Advance reservations are highly recommended. Several different tours are available ranging from a short 45-minute event to more involved historical tours. **www.VeuveClicquot.com**
Vranken Pommery 	5 Place du Général Gouraud, 51100 Reims Group tours and self-guided tours are available and a mobile app for this is provided but headphones are suggested. This is a large facility which often is decorated with light shows and modern art. Included with the visit to the cellars is a champagne museum of Reims. Champagne is produced under both separate labels for Vranken and for Pommery. One caution, this is popular with bus tours so it can get crowded. Open Sunday to Thursday from 10AM to 6PM and until 7PM Friday and Saturday. **www.VrankenPommery.com**

Champagne Houses South of Central Reims	
House/Label	**Address & Details**
Champaign Ruinart	4 Rue des Crayères, 51100 Reims
	Reservations are required for tours into the chalk cellars. This is a 2-hour tour and group sizes are kept small.
	In addition to wine tours, they also offer an added brunch which is done in an elegant setting. This is one of the more expensive champagne tours in Reims.
	Closed Tuesday and Wednesday. Other days, the shop and tours are open from 9:30AM to 5PM.
	www.Ruinart.com

8: Reims Shopping & Dining Areas

One of the great pleasures when exploring a city new to you is to use shopping as a reason or excuse to discover the city's streets and neighborhoods. In Reims, there is a good array of shopping within an easy walk from either the train station or the cathedral area.

While shopping can be found throughout this city, there are four areas which are suggested here. In each case, these include a variety of stores along with restaurants. These shopping areas are almost always a good opportunity to combine dining with shopping.

The areas detailed here range from a popular open market to upscale shopping streets which include notable department stores like the Galleries Lafayette.

The map on the next page highlights the locations of these noteworthy shopping areas in Reims.

Shopping for Champagne?

See chapter 7 for guidance on the more notable champagne houses to visit, taste, and purchase local champagne and wines.

~ ~ ~ ~ ~ ~

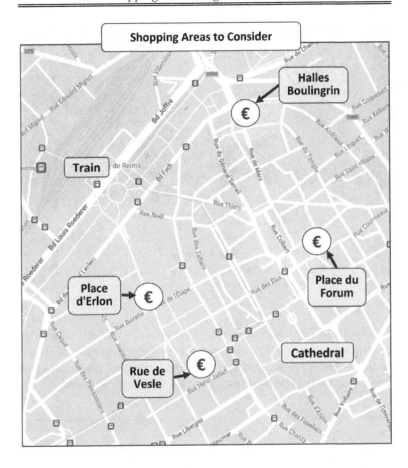

Rue de Vesle: Running southwest a block from the cathedral is the popular shopping street of Rue de Vesle. This is not a tourist-oriented shopping street. It is where the locals go to shop as it includes a variety of trendy boutiques and even major department stores such as Galleries Lafayette and H & M Department Stores.

> **Rue de Vesle** is your best bet for clothing, perfumes, and department stores.

Rue du Vesle
A great street for shopping in the heart of Reims.
Photo source: Poudou99 - Wikimedia Commons

The tram lines run down the center of this street which, in length, it is a bit over ½ mile long. The closer you are to the cathedral, the better the shopping is. This street runs all the way to the canal, but there is little of interest in the section near there.

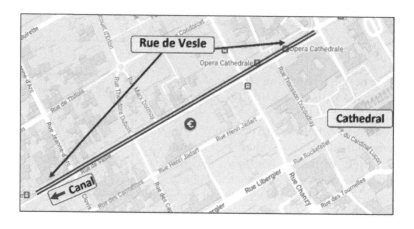

Place d'Erlon (Place Drouet d'Erlon): Close to the train station is a popular area for dining and finding small boutiques.

> Come to **Place d'Erlon** for small boutiques and many quality restaurants.

This is largely a pedestrian-only section, and it is a set of tree-lined boulevards with small shops and restaurants. A great spot for outdoor dining. There are even several small hotels here.

Place Drouet d'Erlon with the Subé Fountain in the center.
Photo Source: Google Maps

Some of the more notable shops specialize in chocolates, jewelry, clothing, and souvenirs.

The focal point of this section of town, as shown on the following map, is the intersection of Place Drouet d'Erlon and Rue de l'Étape. Both of these streets are lined with shops and restaurants for about two blocks in every direction. This area is about a 5-minute walk south from the main Reims train station or, if you are coming here from the cathedral area, plan on a walk of 6 to 8 minutes.

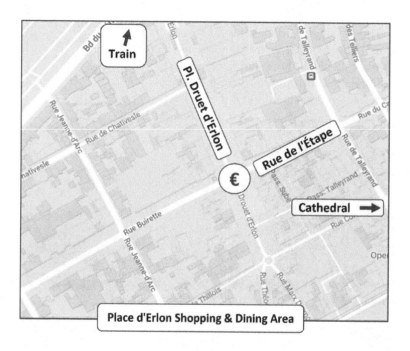

Place d'Erlon Shopping & Dining Area

Halles du Boulingrin: (Also referred to as Halles Centrales de Reims) This is an indoor farmers market inside of a large hangar-like building. Crafted in the Art Deco style, popular when it was built in the 1920's, this is a great place to sample local produce.

> Come to **Halles du Boulingrin** for local produce, baked goods, sweets, and wine.

Cautions: This is not a neighborhood which lends itself to tourism or casual strolling. Also, the hours are limited, and it is not open every day. As of this writing, the hours are:

- Wednesday from 7am to 1pm
- Friday from 7am to 1pm and then later from 4pm to 8pm
- Saturday from 6am to 2pm.

Address: 50 Rue de Mars, 51100 Reims. This is about a 15-minute walk northwest from the cathedral area.

Website: **www.MarcheDuBoulingrin.fr**

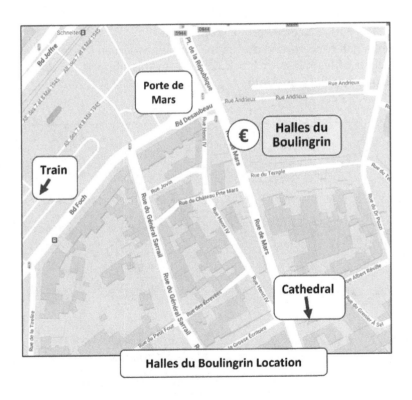

Halles du Boulingrin Location

~ ~ ~ ~ ~ ~

Place du Forum: Located just a short walk north from the Cathedral and nearby Place Royale is Place du Forum. It is a small city park with many areas and tables to relax and enjoy a meal from one of the adjacent restaurants or boulangeries. This is not a shopping haven per se, but it is a good place for relaxed strolling with several popular bars, food shops, and restaurants.

> Come to **Place du Forum** mostly for its restaurants and bars.

The park, Place du Forum, is often a site for small concerts and during the Christmas season it is an active center of festivities. A block north from this plaza is the Reims Hôtel de Ville (City Hall).

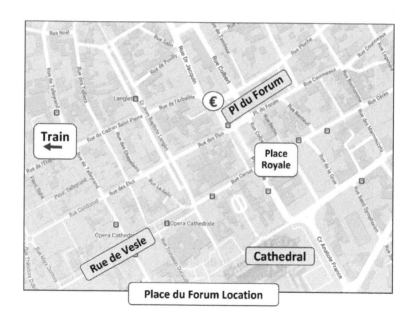

Place du Forum Location

~ ~ ~ ~ ~ ~

9: Épernay Overview & Champagne Houses

One word can define Épernay, a laid-back town of 25,000 people...**champagne.**

Exploring this city is easy as most of what you will want to see is on the one-kilometer-long **Avenue de Champagne**. Along this

lane, there are several world-renowned champagne houses such as Moët Chandon and even a museum devoted to champagne.

Avenue de Champagne - The Richest Street in the World

This 1 km boulevard is often referred to as the richest street in the world due to the over 100km of tunnels under here which hold around 200 million bottles of champagne!

While there are other attractions here such as "Le Balloon" and the Champagne Museum, the focus is on this one beverage. This is an easy town to explore in one day and is a simple day trip from Reims or Paris. As shown in chapter 12, there are many available one-day tours to the Épernay area from Paris.

Épernay also makes a good basecamp for exploring the vineyard-covered hillsides and neighboring villages. Consider, for example, exploring the area by bicycle and stopping along the way at one of the many vineyards.

If you visit by train, it is a short walk of 6 to 8 minutes to the Avenue de Champagne and the town's tourist office. This office is a great place to begin your explorations as they will be up to date on current events and available tours both in town and around the area.

www.Epernay-Tourisme.com

If you are likely to visit several champagne houses, acquiring a Reims-Épernay pass from this tourist office can be beneficial as most of them provide a discount to pass holders. Discounts typically range from 10 to 20% for tastings which, if you visit multiple locations, can quickly add up.

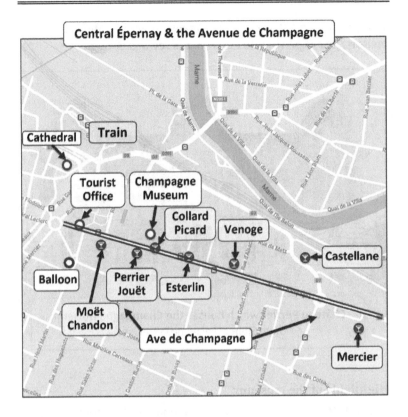

Central Épernay & the Avenue de Champagne

Champagne Museum / Musée du vin de Champagne et d'Archéologie Régionale:

If your schedule allows, coming to this multi-faceted museum should be done before heading off to any of the neighboring champagne houses. It is a great way to learn more about the area and champagne production. This museum also includes a set of caves/cellars under the building and grounds.

This museum is often referred to as Château Perrier as it is housed in the magnificent mansion built for Charles Perrier in

1856. No direct relationship to Perrier mineral water. For many visitors, just exploring this mansion is reward enough.

Château Perrier which houses the Champagne Museum
Photo Source: Palauenc05-Wikipedia

Highlights of the museum:

- Over 2,000 exhibits on the region and its geography.
- Creation and the history of champagne
- Interactive, self-guided tours
- Expansive gardens
- Champagne cellar/caves.

Address: 13, Avenue de Champagne, 51200 Épernay

Hours: Closed on Tuesday. Other days from 10 AM to 7 PM with slightly shorter hours during winter.

Website: ArcheoChampagne.Epernay.Fr

Le Balloon d'Épernay:

An icon of Épernay is the large white balloon which offers visitors the chance to rise high above town. It offers great views of the town, the Avenue de Champagne, and the surrounding vineyard-covered hillsides.

This attraction is one block south of the Ave.de Champagne and hard to miss. Hours are seasonal so check ahead before attempting a ride. This is a tethered balloon which goes straight up from the heart of town and does not float freely, making it a safe ride.

The trip takes a maximum of 29 visitors up at a time and ascends 490 feet (150 meters). Full details may be found on their website at: **www.Balloon-Epernay.com.**

The cost, as of early 2023, is € 14 per adult and € 7 for children.

Avenue de Champagne Houses to Visit:

While the area has numerous champagne houses ranging from boutique to major producers, the grouping along Épernay's Avenue de Champagne should be your starting point. These labels are some of the best in the world and several provide in-depth tours with tastings. This is a relaxing avenue to stroll along and quite a treat to have so many champagne houses within an easy walk from each other.

> **Caution:**
> Some of these champagne houses require reservations or are limited to pre-arranged tour groups. Chapter 12 provides assistance with this.

Épernay Champagne Houses[7]	
House/Label	**Address & Details**
Moët et Chandon	20 Ave. De Champagne, 51200 Épernay
	This is easy to reach as it is across the street from the tourist office and the champagne museum.
	Advance reservations via their website are required and they book up quickly. There are two tour options which vary only by the provided tastings. Tours take visitors deep into the champagne caves.
	www.Moet.com

[7] **Champagne House Listings**: The table lists these houses starting toward the center of town (west) and then moves east to the houses slightly further from town center.

Épernay Champagne Houses[7]	
House/Label	**Address & Details**
Perrier-Jouët	26 Ave. de Champagne, 51200 Épernay One of the more expensive labels but a great tasting experience in a beautiful garden area. This facility is more about tastings and light dining than providing tours. Reservations for tastings are not required. **www.Perrier-Jouet.com**
Collard-Picard	15 Ave. de Champagne, 51200 Épernay The focus is on tastings and not tours here. There is an inviting patio to enjoy the champagne and light snacks. Reservations are not needed. Hours: Open daily from 10AM to 6PM **www.ChampagneCollardPicard.fr**
Esterlin	25 Ave. de Champagne, 51200 Épernay Tastings in a formal setting in a beautiful mansion. Limited tours are provided. Blind tastings are a fun option to try out different varieties. Hours: closed Saturday and Sunday. Weekdays open from 8:30AM to 5PM. Closed for lunch. **www.Champagne-Esterlin.com**

Épernay Champagne Houses[7]	
House/Label	**Address & Details**
Champagne de Venoge	33 Ave. de Champagne, 51200 Épernay In addition to excellent champagne, de Venoge is located in a beautiful 19th-century mansion. Different tour packages are available, and all include a guided tour of the mansion, the cellars and gardens, including multiple tastings. This is also a small hotel which provides guests with the ability to stay in the luxury mansion. **www.ChampagneDeVenoge.com**
Champagne De Castellane	63 Ave. de Champagne, 51200 Épernay Although the address shows them on Ave de Champagne, it is actually one block north on Rue de Verdun. One of the larger champagne houses in the area, it is easy to find due to the tall towers above the facility. Visitors may go to the top of the tower for great views. Several tour options are available including private tours. A relatively affordable tour of a very large facility. Reservations are not required but advised. Caution, this locale can be crowded with bus tour groups. Open every day from 10AM to 6PM **www.Castellane.com**

Épernay Champagne Houses[7]	
House/Label	**Address & Details**
Champagne Mercier	68 Ave. de Champagne, 51200 Épernay
	This is the furthest from town center of the champagne houses listed here but is well worth the trip.
	Visit the champagne cellars via a fun electric train. Different tour options available and advance reservations not required but are advised.
	Hours and days open vary by the season, so check their website before visiting. Caution, this is a popular destination for bus tour groups.
	www.ChampagneMercier.com

10: Lodging in Reims & Épernay

A quick qualifier…it would take a guide far larger than this to detail all of the lodging options in and near Reims or Épernay.[8] The focus is on hotels and large inns within these two towns.

Additional research is advised, especially if you are driving and have the opportunity to stay out of town and in the heart of the Champagne district. This chapter does provide representative examples of some of the area's notable resorts, but this is only a sampling. Resources such as Trip Advisor, Booking.com, or others will do a far more complete job of providing current and comprehensive information, along with reviews on every property in the area.

Author's Recommendation:

If you are coming by **train** and staying for multiple nights, pick lodging in central Reims.

If you are coming for just one night and are focused on champagne, pick lodging in Épernay.

If you are **driving** (and can afford it), pick one of the resorts near town.

---

[8] **Geographical Limitation**: Champagne is a large area which covers many towns, villages, and growing areas. This guide is focused on Reims, Épernay, and some noteworthy resorts between these two towns. This is not a comprehensive lodging guide to the entire Champagne area.

Hotels in Central Reims:

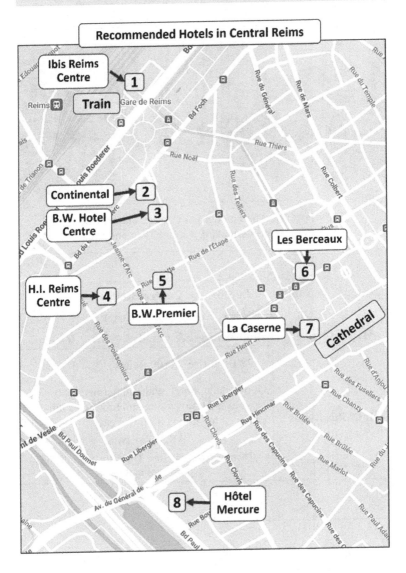

Recommended Hotels in Central Reims

**Marriott's new and modern La Caserne Chanzy Hotel
provides rooms overlooking the cathedral and square.**

Suggested Lodging in Central Reims		
(All selected lodging has 3.5 or better rating)[9]		
Map # & Hotel	**Address & Details**	**Rating**
-1- **Hôtel ibis Reims Centre**	28 Bd Joffre, 51100 Reims $\quad$ 3.5 stars Good chain hotel with numerous amenities. Next to the train station and tram lines into the center of town making travel easy. **All.Accor.com** Then search for Reims. There are multiple ibis properties in Reims.	

---

[9] **Hotel Ratings:** Ratings cited in this guide are a composite of author's experience and other rating sources such as Trip Advisor, Google, Booking.com. No one single source was used.

Map # & Hotel	Address & Details	Rating
Suggested Lodging in Central Reims (All selected lodging has 3.5 or better rating)[9]		
-2- **Continental Hotel Reims**	93 Pl. Drouet d'Erlon, 51100 Reims	4 stars
	Perfectly located near the train station and adjacent to the Place Drouet d'Erlon shopping and dining street. Many large rooms and a well-rated restaurant. Parking is available if you are driving. **www.Continental-Hotel.fr** (Not an Intercontinental Hotel)	
-3- **Best Western Hôtel Centre Reims**	75 Pl. Drouet d'Erlon, 51100 Reims	3.5 stars
	Near-perfect location next to shopping and dining and easy walk to the train and center of town. Sizeable rooms. One caution, rooms facing the street can be noisy until very late. **www.Hotel-Centre-Reims.fr** Note: This is not the only Best Western in the area. The Best Western Premier is another option nearby.	
-4- **Holiday Inn Reims Centre**	46 Rue Buirette, 51100 Reims	4 stars
	Check out the roof-top dining area and bar for great views of the area. Modern hotel with large rooms. A bit of a walk to the center of town and few restaurants in the neighborhood. If you are driving, there is parking available, and the property is pet friendly. **www.IHG.com** Then search for Reims.	

Map # & Hotel	Address & Details	Rating
-5- **Best Western Premier Hotel De La Paix**	9 Rue Buirette, 51100 Reims	4 stars
	Large, modern hotel which is well located for shopping, dining, and an easy walk into the cathedral area. On a quiet street which is lined with restaurants. Full service with conference facilities and indoor pool. **www.BestWestern-Lapaix-Reims.com** This is not the only Best Western in the area.	
-6- **Les Berceaux de la Cathedrale**	2 Rue JB et AR de la Salle, 51100 Reims	4.5 stars
	Boutique property which is more small apartments than hotel. Great views of the cathedral and right in the heart of town. Modern 1-bedroom apartments with kitchens and sitting areas. **www.Les-Berceaux-De-La-Cathedrale.com**	
-7- **La Caserne Chanzy Hôtel & Spa**	18 Rue Tronsson Docoudray, 51100 Reims	5 stars
	Author favorite. A Marriott Autograph Hotel. New, modern, and next to the cathedral. Large rooms, full-service property, and excellent service. A bit pricey but, if your budget allows, consider staying here. **www.LaCaserneChanzy.com** Or find the property on Marriott.com	

Suggested Lodging in Central Reims

(All selected lodging has 3.5 or better rating)[9]

Suggested Lodging in Central Reims		
(All selected lodging has 3.5 or better rating)[9]		
Map # & Hotel	**Address & Details**	**Rating**
-8- **Hôtel Mercure Reims Centre Cathédrale**	31 Bd Paul Doumer, 51100 Reims	4 stars
	This is a very large hotel with full facilities including parking, restaurant, and bar. It is the only property listed here on the river and can be enjoyable to stroll along. To get into town, it is a 10+ minute walk and is not as close to the cathedral area as the property name implies. **All.Accor.com** Then search for Reims and select this property.	

The Hôtel Mercure Reims Centre Cathédrale

~ ~ ~ ~ ~ ~

Hotels in Central Épernay:

Staying in the heart of Épernay is often characterized by upscale or small boutique inns, some of which are more B-and-B than they are hotels. In almost every case, champagne is a central element and tastings will often be provided.

Most central Épernay inns are along the noted Avenue de Champagne which is a relaxed environment. This is not an area to expect to find numerous shops, bars and restaurants close to your lodging. Dining within the hotel is often your best choice or a long walk may be in order.

Seven properties are outlined here as they are all well rated and provide a pleasant experience. There are also several resorts and inns outside of town, some of which are adjacent to vineyards. Several of these are cited in the next section of this chapter.

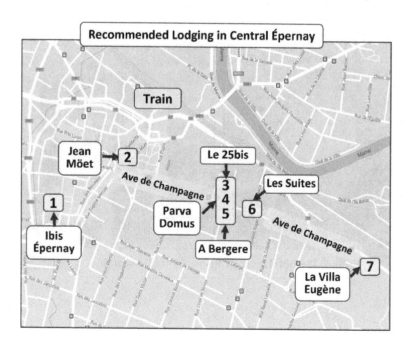

Hôtel Jean Moët, a charming inn near the start of the Ave. de Champagne.

Suggested Lodging in Central Épernay		
(All selected lodging has 3.5 or better rating)[10]		
Map # & Hotel	**Address & Details**	**Rating**
-1- **ibis Épernay** **Centre-Ville**	19 Rue Chocatelle, Pl. Bernard-Stasi, 51200 Épernay	3.5 stars
	This is the largest property on this list, and it is a chain hotel. Near the center of the business district. The one downside is its distance to Ave. de Champagne and access to the train station.	
	All.Accor.com	
	Then search for Épernay	

---

[10] **Hotel Ratings:** Ratings for Épernay hotels and inns cited here are a composite of author's experience and other rating sources such as Trip Advisor, Google, and Booking.com. No one single source was used.

Suggested Lodging in Central Épernay

(All selected lodging has 3.5 or better rating)[10]

Map # & Hotel	Address & Details	Rating
-2- **Hôtel Jean Moët**	7 Rue Jean Moët, 51200 Épernay 4 stars A boutique hotel with a great patio to enjoy brunch and champagne. Extremely well located at the start of Ave. de Champagne and a short walk to the train station. The rooms are modern and fairly large. **www.HotelJeanMoet.com**	
-3- **Le 25bis by Leclerc Briant**	25 bis Av de Champagne 4.5 stars A small bed and breakfast located in a classic mansion and champagne house. Located in the center of Ave. de Champagne. Quiet luxury and superior service. **www.Le25Bis.com**	
-4- **Parva Domus Chambres d'Hotes**	27 Av de Champagne 4 stars Tucked back from the Ave. de Champagne, it would be easy to miss this quaint B & B. It is not large, but it provides a quality stay and great breakfast. The front patio is a perfect place to relax with a glass of their champagne. **www.ParvaDomusRimaire.com**	
-5- **Champagne A Bergère**	40 Av de Champagne, 4 stars As with several other properties here, this is a combination champagne house and inn. Stay in a former mansion. Rooms are well-sized and nicely decorated. **www.Champagne-ABergere.com**	

Suggested Lodging in Central Épernay		
(All selected lodging has 3.5 or better rating)[10]		
Map # & Hotel	**Address & Details**	**Rating**
-6- **Les Suites du 33**	40 Av de Champagne 　　　　 4 stars A beautiful mansion with contemporary décor. Connected to the Champagne de Venoge house so some confusion with the site's name may occur. Kitchenettes are included and the suites are large. **www.ChampagneDeVenoge.com**	
-7- **La Villa Eugène**	Av de Champagne, 51200 Épernay 　　 4.5 stars A downside to this beautiful boutique hotel is its distance from the heart of town. A walk of 10+ minutes is needed to reach the town center. Full amenities, even a swimming pool. Luxurious décor, grounds, and rooms. A bit pricey. **www.Villa-Eugene.com**	

Dining area in La Villa Eugène - a luxury inn near the end of the Ave. de Champagne.
Photo Source: Villa-Eugene.com

Inns & Resorts Between Reims and Épernay:

This is champagne country, so consider staying in lodging surrounded by vineyards, beautiful rolling hills, and small villages.

The entire champagne region, which goes well beyond the two towns of Reims and Épernay, is dotted with lodging opportunities ranging from small guest houses to magnificent resorts. Staying in one of these often provides the opportunity to get out and explore the area, vineyards, and trails on bicycle or foot. Much of this area is inside of the large "**Parc Naturel Régional de la Montagne**" which provides a wealth of beautiful open country to explore.

The following are several of the more notable properties to consider in the area immediately adjacent to Reims and Épernay, but this is a representative sampling only. Greater research on such sites as Trip Advisor is recommended.

The Royal Champagne Hotel and Spa
5-star luxury overlooking vineyards just north of Épernay.

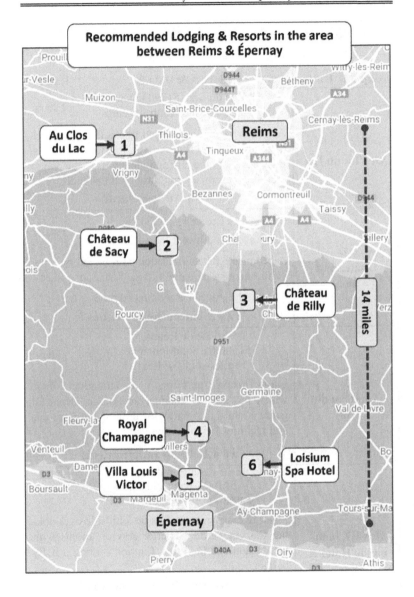

Recommended Lodging & Resorts in the area between Reims & Épernay

Map # & Hotel	Address & Details	Rating
Suggested Lodging between Reims and Épernay (All selected lodging has 3.5 or better rating)		
-1- **Au Clos du Lac**	18 Rue du Lac, 51390 Gueux 4 ½ miles west of central Reims A former farmhouse turned into a B & B, which includes pool and fitness areas, just west of Reims. Easy access to the city and vineyards. Take one of their bicycles on a jaunt through the village. **www.Auclosdulac.fr**	4 stars
-2- **Château de Sacy**	Rue des Croisettes, 51500 Sacy 5 miles southwest from Reims A beautiful château/mansion surrounded by vineyards and near a quaint village. 5-star amenities. Author Recommendation **www.ChateauDeSacy-Reims.fr**	5 stars
-3- **Château de Rilly**	38 Rue de Reims, 51500 Rilly-laMontagne 5 miles south of Reims Large, historic mansion in an attractive village which has several champagne houses. Beautiful gardens and large patio for dining. Large rooms and facilities include a spa. **www.LeChateauDeRilly.com**	5 stars
-4- **Royal Champagne Hotel & Spa**	9 Rue de la République 51160 Champillon 3 miles north of Épernay 5-star in every regard. Sits on a hillside overlooking the vineyards. Superior service, rooms with views, and spa facilities. Caution – bring a hefty budget. **www.RoyalChampagne.com**	5 stars

Suggested Lodging between Reims and Épernay

(All selected lodging has 3.5 or better rating)

Map # & Hotel	Address & Details	Rating
-5- **Villa Louis Victor**	557 Av. du Général Leclerc 51530 Dizy 1 1/2 miles north of Épernay A quiet B & B in the center of a suburb just north of Épernay. The neighborhood has little to offer, but the rooms in the inn are large and suites are available. Easy parking if you are driving. **www.Villa-LouisVictor.com**	3.5 stars
-6- **Losium Wine & Spa Hôtel**	1 Allée de la Sapinière 51160 Mutigny 3 1/2 miles northeast of Épernay A perfect setting in the country, overlooking vineyards in one direction and backed by forest. Large, modern and new facility with 5-star service, rooms, and amenities. **www.Losium.com**	5 stars

~ ~ ~ ~ ~ ~

11: The Champagne Routes

The Champagne area, with its rolling hills, forests, villages, and vineyards is beautiful. It is also quite large. One great way to explore these bucolic treasures is to drive some of the Champagne Route, or "**Route Touristique du Champagne**."[11]

While this "route" is often referrred to in the singular, it is actually a set of several differing routes, each with their own charm. Four of these routes connect to the small cities of Reims and Épernay and they are outlined in this chapter.

Route markers are present and will help you find your way. Two quick cautions when planning on visiting the area: (a) self driving or guided tours are needed, and (b) many of the champagne houses require advance reservations.

[11] **Recommended Champagne Region Website**: The following website is one of the better resources for local information and details on the best champagne houses here. It is a great planning tool to use prior to driving any portion of this route. **www.Tourisme-en-Champagne.com**.

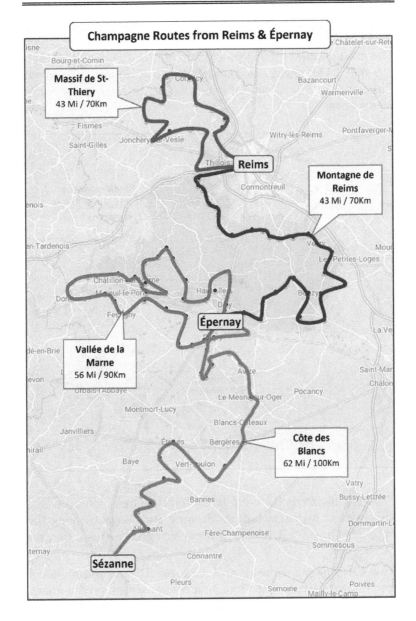

Montagne de Reims / Mountain of Reims:

The most popular route segment and for good reason. Although it is only 24 kilometers as a straight line from Reims to Épernay, this route is a full 70km as it winds its way through many of the area's towns.

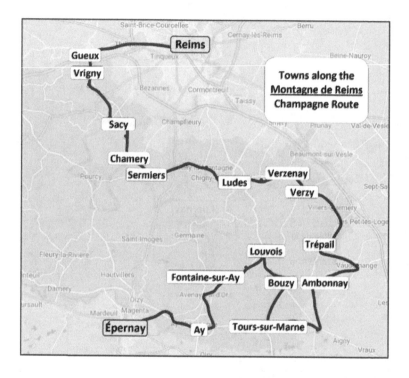

Along the route there are large, forested areas and attractive villages and towns including Mutigny and Verzy. Among the highlights here is a lighthouse from which great views of the area can be seen.

The Champagne Houses and Grapes: The most prominent grapes here are reds with Pinot Noir being the most predominant. Chardonnay accounts for roughly a third of the area planted.

Champagne houses here range from small, family-run operations to large world-renown labels such as Bollinger. Thirty of the champagne houses here have been awarded the Vignobles & Découvertes[12] designation.

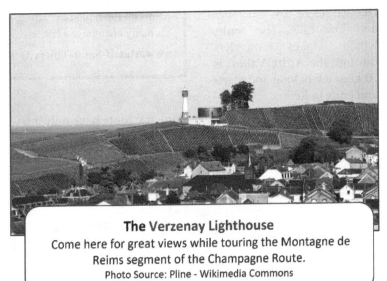

The Verzenay Lighthouse
Come here for great views while touring the Montagne de Reims segment of the Champagne Route.
Photo Source: Pline - Wikimedia Commons

Bottom-Line: This is a great segment of the champagne route to visit and there are many well-rated champagne houses which do not require advance reservations. If you can tour only one part of the champagne route, consider this one.

---

[12] **Vignobles & Découvertes** This is a designation granted by the France Tourism board to wineries who not only produce a superior product but also professionally and openly engage with visitors and tourists to help them understand the art and history of wine making.

Massif de St. Thiery:

This is the northernmost section of the Champagne region and is an area characterized by marshes and low hills. The route, which takes travelers through the Ardre Valley, is 70 kilometers long and starts and ends in Reims.

Website Resource:
The following site provides details on the region including its many champagne houses.
www.Massif-Saint-Thiery.fr

Most of the towns and villages along the route have only a few hundred inhabitants. The focal point of each of these villages is agriculture, which includes wine growing.

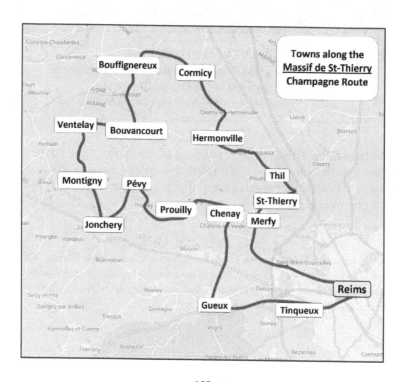

Towns along the
Massif de St-Thierry
Champagne Route

Bouffignereux
Cormicy
Ventelay
Bouvancourt
Hermonville
Montigny
Pévy
Thil
St-Thierry
Prouilly
Chenay
Merfy
Jonchery
Reims
Gueux
Tinqueux

One highlight along this drive is the Abbey of Saint Thierry. This is a previous residence of the bishops of Champagne which was founded around the year 500.

Champagne Houses & Vintners: This area is noted for its red wines such as Pinot-Noir which lean toward fruity tones. Many of the champagne houses are smaller, independent operations and, as a result, do not have large facilities for tastings and tours.

Bottom-Line: This is a pleasant area to drive through with attractive small villages but is not conducive to touring champagne houses in a casual manner without advance planning. Consider not making this segment of the Champagne Routes your first choice.

Vallée de la Marne / Marne Valley:

This 90-kilometer loop largely runs along the Marne River east from Épernay. There are 25 champagne cellars along the route

The Vallée de la Marne is characterized by low hills and numerous villages surrounded by vineyards such as Troissy shown here.

which carry the V & D label, (Vignobles & Découvertes) which means they provide quality products and service.

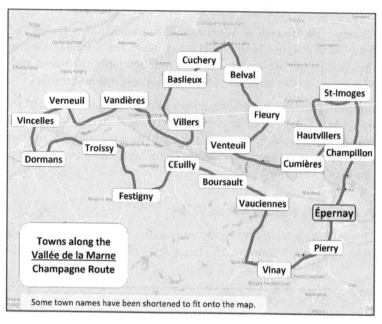

Some town names have been shortened to fit onto the map.

Among the region's more attractive villages is Hautvillers, a picturesque locale which was the home of the monk Dom Pérignon, the creator of champagne. In the town of Dormans there is an impressive war memorial to the WWI battle of Marne.

Bottom-Line: You can't go wrong with a tour along this loop. Starting and ending in Épernay makes planning easy. Along the route the scenery is what you would want when traveling through the Champagne region and there are numerous attractive villages along the way to add to your day.

~ ~ ~ ~ ~ ~

Côte des Blancs:

This area, (Loosely translated as the hillsides of white wines) is the birthplace of Chardonnay wine. Chardonnay grapes account for 97% of wine production here.

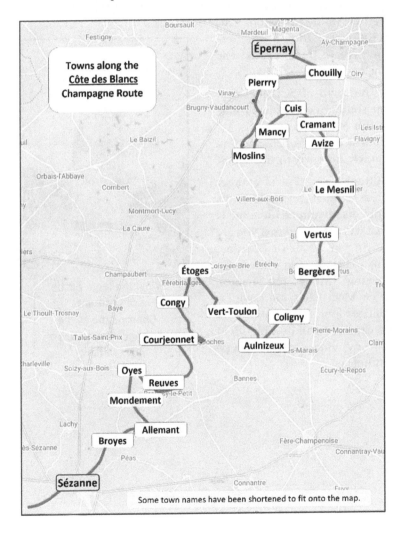

The route meanders 100 kilometers south from Épernay and takes visitors to and slightly beyond the medieval town and Sézanne. Some resources will refer to this route as **the Coteaux du Sézzanis.**

One popular stop is Mont Aimé, a promontory near the town of Vertus (mid-way along the route). In addition to great views there are remnants of an ancient castle.

The town of Sézanne, near the southern end of this route, is fun to explore with its ancient streets, a Renaissance era church and early fortifications.

Bottom-Line: This is another great stretch to explore. Its only disadvantage for some is that it is not a loop so if you are staying in Reims or Épernay, this may generate some extra driving. Many top names, even Moet Chandon have facilities along the route. A visit to Cramant will be a highlight for any wine and champagne enthusiast.

View the large bottle of Cramant Champagne at the entrance to the town of Cramant.

~ ~ ~ ~ ~ ~

12: Reims, Épernay & Champagne Tours

While many individuals prefer to manage visits to a new town or wine area on their own, there is a lot to say for joining a tour as the tour company can take you into champagne houses which might otherwise be closed to single visitors, and they will provide a wealth of local information.

In the case of visiting the Champagne area, the opportunities go well beyond quick trips out from Reims or Épernay. There are also options for visiting here from Paris as well and, in some cases, these are multi-day, emersive experiences.

In almost every case, the focus will be on visiting leading champagne houses in the area. Some tours will also include visits to area WWI battlefields.

As a caution, when visiting champagne houses, especially the more notable names, **reservations are often required.**

This chapter provides initial guidance on:

- Booking your own tastings and wine tours
- Champagne tours from Reims and Épernay
- Champagne tours from Paris

Booking Champagne Tours and Tastings on Your Own:

Many of us prefer to go solo when doing such activities as taking a wine tour or visiting a champagne house or vineyard. Unfortunately, many of the area champagne houses require advance booking and do not provide much help on their websites. Another situation is that several of the more popular champagne houses don't require advance reservations but are known to fill up quickly, reducing your opportunity to visit them.

The solution is to use one of the leading services such as **Rue des Vignerons** or **Champagne Booking**. These helpful programs are available via their website and on their apps. The programs include:

- Details on leading vintners throughout France which includes the Champagne district. (Most, not all, of the champagne houses listed in this guide are included in this app.)

Consider downloading the
Rue des Vignerons
app to book champagne house tours.

- Book wine and champagne tours, tastings and workshops.

www.RueDesVignerons.com
(Then select English and pick the Champagne section of the site or app)

or

www.Champagne-Booking.com
(This program has the advantage of focusing on Reims and Épernay)

Champagne Tours from Reims & Épernay:

Given the popularity of touring the Champagne area, it will come as no surprise to learn that numerous companies exist to help in this regard. These range from small operators to international firms such as Viator or Get Your Guide.

There is a substantial overlap in tours sold through these agencies and prices tend to be the same or similar so some comparison shopping may be in order. Details on some of the leading area tour companies follow.

Winegrower For A Day
One of several fun experience-tours offered by the Reims Tourist Office.

Tourist Offices for Reims and Épernay. Local tourist offices are often the best place to check for locally provided tours and the towns of Reims and Épernay are no exception.

In addition to assisting with tasting tours several unique offerings are available from here such as:

- Private and group tours to area vineyards
- Champagne tasting classes
- Be a winegrower for a day
- Cathedral Tours
- Walking Tours of central Reims

Websites for these tourist offices are:

- <u>Reims</u>: **en.Reims-Tourisme.com**
- <u>Épernay</u>: **www.Epernay-Tourisme.com**

The Champagne Tour Company: www.Champagne-Tour.com.
A Reims-based agency which specializes in champagne tours and tastings. All tours are private so, as a result, they can be a bit pricey. Half and full-day tours are available out of Reims, Épernay and Paris.

The company lets you select the amount of time you wish to devote to champagne tours and to historic sites. Specialty tours to noted houses such as Dom Perignon or Veuve Clicquot are also available.

Tours By Locals: www.ToursByLocals.com (Then search for Reims or Épernay)

This is a nationwide tour provider which uses the theme of hiring local individuals to run tours for them. There are a limited number of available tours in the Champagne area ranging from small group to private tours. There are even multi-day tours available. An excellent resource to work with to help ensure you have a great trip.

The one downside is their tours tend to be expensive. A full-day, small-group tour of Reims and the Marne Valley, for example, will be over € 2,000 for a private group.

Viator: www.Viator.com or www.TripAdvisor.com. Viator is a subset of the popular Trip Advisor program. They do not offer their own tours but, rather, resell a host of available tours from local providers. There are many to choose with them. A strength of this firm is excellent customer service. [13]

Consider booking a champagne vineyard bicycle tour with Viator or one of several other operators.

Tours available in the Champagne region are available for most budgets and will range from large bus tours to private events. At the very least, consider simply browsing through their website to obtain some tour ideas as there are many to select from.

---

[13] **Other tour resellers like Viator**: Many other firms also resell these tours like this such as GetYourGuide.com / Visit A City, Booking.com and others so if you have a preferred source for reserving hotels and tours, then in all probability you can use them for many available tours in and around Reims.

Champagne Tours from Paris:

In addition to making your own travel arrangements to Reims or Épernay from Paris, which is easy to do, there are many tour operators available who can remove all hassle. These tours will always be a full day and many are multi-day.

One thing to watch for when selecting a tour is the pick-up and drop-off point in Paris. Private tours will often come directly to your Paris lodging while larger bus groups will depart from a designated central point, typically near the 1st arr.

The list of operators is very similar to the providers for tours which start in Reims but there are a few which specialize in providing tours to the Champagne region from Paris.

Some of the leading providers include:

- My Wine Days – **www.MyWineDays.com**

- Wine Tours Paris – **www.WineToursParis.com**

- Viator – **www.Viator.com**

- Ger Your Guide – **www.GetYourGuide.com**

~ ~ ~ ~ ~ ~

119

Appendix: Websites for Additional Information

To help you expand your knowledge of this area, several online reference sites are listed here. Reims and the Champagne area have a wealth of online references and tourism sites which can help in planning your trip.

The following is a list of online references for this city and the area. The purpose of this list is to enhance your understanding before embarking on your trip. Any online search will result in the websites outlined here plus many others. These are listed as they are professionally done and do not only try to sell you tours.

1-Reims, Épernay & Champagne Region Websites.	
Website Name	**Website address and description**
About France	**www.About-France.com** – then search for Reims or Champagne. Overview of the Champagne region, history, villages, wine tasting, and top attractions throughout the area.
Reims Tourism	**en.Reims-Tourisme.com** Details on the city of Reims, hotels, activities, champagne tours.

1-Reims, Épernay & Champagne Region Websites.	
Website Name	**Website address and description**
Épernay Tourism	**www.Epermay-Tourisme.com** Guidance for visiting Épernay, and information on area tours, champagne tastings and lodging.
Visit Champagne	**www.Tourisme-en-Champagne.com** A great overview of champagne, the beverage and details on the area. Check out the "Visit Champagne" section. This site also provides some guidance on the various Champagne routes.
Reims & Épernay Pass	**www.Reims-Epernay-Pass.com** Pass providing discounts to champagne tastings and free entry to area museums.
Reims City Attractions	**www.Reims.fr** and **www.Musees-Reims.fr** Both sites provide details on the city of Reims and attractions such as the cathedral and museums.
Union des Maisons de Champagne	**www.Maisons-Champagne.com/en** Similar to the Visit Champagne site, this site focuses on area champagne houses and cellar visits. Excellent details on each growing area.
Châlons-en-Champagne Tourist Office	**www.Chalons-Tourisme.com/en** If you will be visiting Chalons, (The town is not detailed in this guide) this site will help you gain an appreciation of the town.

1-Reims, Épernay & Champagne Region Websites.	
Website Name	**Website address and description**
Trip Advisor	**www.TripAdvisor.com** – then search for Reims or other town of interest. One of the best overall travel sights with details and reviews on most attractions, restaurants, and hotels.
Wine Folly	**www.WineFolly.com** Guide to all wine areas including Champagne. A great resource to learn more about how the grapes are harvested and which labels are best.

2-Transportation Information and Tickets	
Website Name	**Website Address & Description**
Citura – Reims Transportation	**www.Citura.fr** Reims bus and tram website and app. Detailed routes and ability to purchase transportation passes.
Oui Bike	**www.OuiBike.net** Bicycle rental service in Reims and several other area cities.
ZébullO	**www.Reims.fr** The bikeshare program in Reims with numerous stations throughout the city. Download the app if you will be renting bikes while in Reims.
Rome 2 Rio	**www.Rome2Rio.com** An excellent site for comparing travel times and costs across different modes of transportation. Tickets may be booked from this site.

2-Transportation Information and Tickets	
Website Name	**Website Address & Description**
French Train / SNCF	**www.SNCF.com/en** Book rail tickets directly with French rail lines and find detailed information on time schedules and train availability.
Train Ticket Resellers	Several services enable you to purchase train tickets online prior to your trip, including: - RailEurope.com - TrainLine.com - Eurorailways.com These sites are a good place to check schedules and train availability for all train companies servicing most areas in Europe.

3-Tour and Hotel Booking Sites	
Service	**Website address and description**
Champagne House Tours & Tastings	The following two sites enable you to make reservations for tours of area champagne houses and tastings. Without using one of these, you may find many locations which are not open to your visiting them. - **www.RueDesVigernons.com** - **www.Champagne-Booking.com**

3-Tour and Hotel Booking Sites	
Service	**Website address and description**
Champagne Area Tours	The following small companies provide tours to the Champagne area, including tastings. - **www.Champagne-Tour.com** - **www.MyWineDays.com** - **www.WineToursParis.com**
Hotel Sites	Numerous online sites enable you to review and book hotels online. Most of these sites also resell tours. - Booking.com - Hotels.com - Expedia.com - Travelocity.com
Tour Resellers	Many companies, such as the ones listed here, provide a full variety of tours to Reims and the Champagne area. The offerings are similar, but the research is helpful as some firms offer unique services and tours. - GetYourGuide.com - ToursByLocals.com - Viator.com - WorldTravelGuide.net
Sophies War Tours	**www.SophiesGreatWarTours.com** A Reims based small tour company which specializes in tours of the area's battlefields and monuments.

~ ~ ~ ~ ~ ~

Index of Sights in this Guide

Starting-Point Guides

This guidebook on Reims and Épernay is one of several current and planned *Starting-Point Guides*. Each book in the series is developed with the concept of using one enjoyable city as your basecamp and then exploring from there.

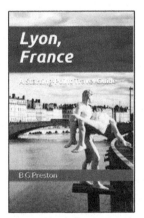

Current guidebooks are for:

- **Bordeaux, France** and the Gironde Region
- **Dijon, France** and the Burgundy Region.
- **Geneva, Switzerland** and the Lake Geneva area.
- **Gothenburg, Sweden** and the central coast of western Sweden.
- **Lille, France** and the Nord-Pas-de-Calais Area
- **Lucerne, Switzerland,** and the Lake Lucerne region.
- **Lyon, France** and the Saône and Rhône confluence area.
- **Nantes, France** and the western Loire Valley
- **Salzburg Austria** and central Austria
- **Strasbourg, France** and the central Alsace area.
- **Stuttgart, Germany** and the Baden-Wurttemberg area.
- **Toledo, Spain** and the Don Quixote route.
- **Toulouse, France,** and the Haute-Garonne region.

Updates on these and other titles may be found on the author's Facebook page at:

www.Facebook.com/BGPreston.author

Feel free to use this Facebook page to provide feedback and suggestions to the author or email to: cincy3@gmail.com

Made in the USA
Las Vegas, NV
06 October 2023